Greg Dombowsky's

DIVER'S GUIDE

Vancouver Island South

Heritage House

Copyright © 1999 Greg Dombowsky

Canadian Cataloguing in Publication Data

Dombowsky, Greg, 1964-
  Diver's guide

  ISBN 1-895811-88-0

  1. Scuba diving—British Columbia—Vancouver Island—
Guidebooks. 2. Vancouver Island (B.C.)—Guidebooks. I. Title.
GV838.673.C3D65 1999   797.2'3   C99-910163-3

First edition 1999

Heritage House wishes to acknowledge the support of Heritage Canada
through the Book Publishing Industry Development Program, the
British Columbia Arts Council, and the Canada Council for the Arts.

Photography, illustrations, and maps by Greg Dombowsky
Design and layout by Darlene Nickull
Edited by Audrey McClellan

HERITAGE HOUSE PUBLISHING COMPANY LTD.
Unit #8 - 17921 55th Ave., Surrey, BC V3S 6C4

Printed in Canada

ACKNOWLEDGEMENTS

MIKE KALINA has been a faithful dive buddy for a long time and was there at a moment's notice whenever I needed to get out. Thank you Mike.

GORD OLIVER gave me a lot of support and patience and was instrumental in the completion of this book.

JACQUES MARC is a member of the Underwater Archaeological Society of BC and his experience was crucial in several of the dive sites.

JIM COSGROVE is a prominent marine biologist in British Columbia. Jim was a great help with the "Marine Life" section in the Introduction of this book.

KEVIN VAN KLEEMPUT'S knowledge of the dive sites and currents around Victoria was a great help.

JASON GALVIN'S artistic talents were used to help me create the maps of the *G.B. Church*.

OLIVER BROST contributed a map of Henderson Point that I used as a basis for my map of that site.

IONNE DOMBOWSKY (my mom) encouraged and helped me in my endeavours.

And last but not least…ANN-MARIE BARRETT supported my efforts all the way and re-inspired me when I needed it.

Disclaimer and limitation of liability

This guidebook is intended to provide recreational divers with information about diving sites discussed in this book in order to help them have an enjoyable time. The information contained in this guidebook is supplied merely for the convenience of the reader. The author has endeavoured to ensure that the information contained in this book is accurate at the time of publication. However, the user is cautioned that this information may be incorrect or incomplete and that it may change after the date of publication. Users of this book and their diving buddies must evaluate for themselves the potential risks and dangers of each site listed in this book, including the availability of adequate or appropriate emergency services.

Neither the publisher, Heritage House Publishing Company Ltd., nor its directors, officers, and employees have adequate scuba diving expertise to confirm the information contained in this guidebook, which is solely within the knowledge of the author. This guidebook is not meant to teach the reader to become a certified scuba diver and it is not meant to be used for non-recreational purposes. Neither the author not the publisher are engaged in providing professional guide services.

This guidebook is sold with the understanding that the author, the bookseller, and the publisher disclaim any responsibility with respect to the completeness or accuracy of the information provided in this guidebook and will not be liable with respect to any claim, action or proceeding relating to any injury, death, loss of property, or damage to property caused or alleged to be caused, directly or indirectly, by the information contained in or omitted from this guidebook whether caused by negligence or otherwise.

We urge you to read the Introduction as it contains information that is essential to understanding the rest of this book. Readers can send corrections, comments, and dive site observations to the author at update@dive.bc.ca. Visit http://dive.bc.ca for more information on diving around Victoria and British Columbia.

CONTENTS

*An asterisk indicates the site is a Top Ten Selection

INTRODUCTION

Thank you for purchasing *Diver's Guide: Vancouver Island South.* I hope you have as much fun using this book to explore the exciting waters around Victoria as I had writing it.

Since I was certified as a PADI (Professional Association of Diving Instructors) Open Water diver in 1990, I've had the opportunity to visit many diving meccas around the world—California, Hawaii, Mexico, Malaysia, Indonesia, and Thailand. My experiences on these travels convince me that the diving in Victoria is among the best in the world.

Skill Levels and Common Sense

In this book I will not go over basic scuba rules that you should already know and skills that you should already have mastered. I do hope that all divers use common sense when it comes to a sport as potentially dangerous as diving. The danger only arises when divers do not follow the rules that they have been taught or do not use common sense.

Under certain conditions, any site can become more than a beginning diver is able to handle. For this reason I have not labelled the sites in this book with a difficulty rating. I consider it every diver's responsibility to know his or her own abilities and limitations. You should also know the abilities and limitations of your diving buddy and make dive site choices that are acceptable to both of you. After reading the information contained in this book and checking the current, visibility, and weather conditions, you should be able to evaluate a dive site to determine its acceptability for you and your buddy.

Marine Life

Most people get interested in diving because of the possibility it offers to encounter marine life or "life" in diver terminology. Seeing the larger animals can be exhilarating for some and scary for others. No matter which category you fall into, your training and common sense will guide you safely through most encounters with marine life.

Even though we do not have coral reefs in Canada, we do have a lot of fragile animals. Fins, gauges, and hands can cause fatal damage to many sea creatures. Our interactions with a marine organism can affect that animal more than we can imagine. Try to keep your impact on all life to a minimum, preferably observation only. Do not attempt to touch any creature as you may harm it or it may harm you.

If you spearfish or harvest seafood, please use some restraint. The following are a few suggestions when collecting:

- Take only what you can personally consume. Most seafood "gifts" go to waste.
- Unless you have a good shot at a fish, don't take it. Injured fish often die.
- Keep up on all the latest regulations in the sport-fishing guide. Even when the season is open for a species, there are often smaller areas that are closed all year.
- Don't harvest from known dive sites.

Invertebrates come in a rainbow of colours and a variety of sizes. There are thousands of different species in British Columbia. Most species filter the water and remove the particles that it contains, but some species, like the starfish, actually attack other animals. Wherever you find strong current, you are likely to find a good selection of invertebrates.

Countless numbers of **fish** species live in our waters, far too many for me to mention. The most commonly seen are ling cod and rockfish. Identifying the fish you see on each dive can be a lot of fun. Most fish guidebooks will refer to the various parts of a fish when describing them. The diagram below shows you what those guides are referring to.

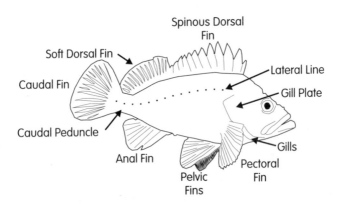

Some of the marine life that you may encounter in the waters around southern Vancouver Island is:

Octopus

The octopuses found in the Pacific Northwest are the largest on earth. Jim Cosgrove, a local marine biologist and octopus expert, has seen an octopus that weighed 70 kilograms (150 pounds) and was 7 metres long (23 feet). Although they can grow to such an enormous size, it is more common for divers to see octopuses from a few centimetres to about a metre in length.

Magicians can't keep up to an octopus when it comes to tricky manoeuvres. Octopuses can change the colour and texture of their skin in seconds in order to blend in and elude predators or ambush prey. Colour change is also used as a form of communication with other octopuses. Another trick is to squirt ink into the water and disappear into a "cloud of smoke." They also use their siphon tubes to jet themselves away.

During the daytime, octopuses usually stay in their dens, which can be recognized by a patch of shells at the entrance. They hunt primarily at night or on dark dreary days, so these are the best times to find them out and about. Octopuses eat a wide variety of things depending on what food is available in their area. Crabs, scallops, cockles, abalone, and most anything with a shell would be on the menu.

Octopuses have many weapons to use on their prey while they are hunting. They use venom to anaesthetize their prey so that they can continue collecting food before they go home and have a feast. Sensory organs on their suckers allow them to smell out prey. If there is a crab under a rock, an octopus can reach in with its arm, smell the crab, and then grab it with powerful arms and suckers. Once it has captured its prey, the octopus uses its powerful beak, much like the beak of a large parrot, to crack the shell. It also has a tongue that serves as a drill when necessary. There are rasps on the end of the tongue, and when the octopus moves it back and forth it creates a hole in a shell that would otherwise be hard to crack.

Octopuses are intelligent, graceful, beautiful creatures. Please don't try to handle them or remove them from their dens.

Ling Cod

For years, ling cod stocks were being depleted and it was becoming less common for divers to see them. Now, however, the ling cod population is coming back strong due to the regulations set forth by the Department of Fisheries and Oceans (DFO).

Ling cod breed during the winter months. Starting around October the male ling cod establishes a territory in the hopes of attracting a female. When a female arrives she deposits her eggs, the male fertilizes them, and then the female leaves. It is the duty of the male to guard the eggs until they hatch. Then he is free to roam until the next winter, when he will do the whole thing over again.

It is common during the winter months to encounter aggressive ling cod protecting their eggs. Although I have never heard of a ling cod hurting anyone, they could startle you.

Sharks

There are numerous shark species in the Pacific Northwest. I have never heard or read of a shark attack in British Columbia waters. However, most sharks found in our waters have teeth and all are potentially dangerous.

Divers most commonly see the spiny dogfish and the six-gill shark. Dogfish are not generally considered dangerous, but if you notice schooling or aggressive behaviour, leave the area. Dogfish grow to a maximum size of 1.5 metres (5 feet).

It is exciting to see six-gill sharks. They are recognizable by their sleek look and their lack of the classic shark-shape dorsal fin. At up to 6 metres (20 feet) in length, they can be quite intimidating. Most sightings in the Victoria area occur at McKenzie Bight in the Saanich Inlet during the summer months.

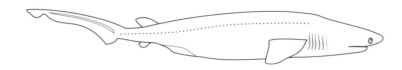

Wolf Eels

Wolf eels can grow to 2 metres (6 feet) long. The males are lighter in colour and have large, bulbous, wrinkly heads. The females have a smaller head, a more streamlined appearance, and are slightly darker.

Many wolf eels that live near common dive sites have become *almost* tame. This is not necessarily a good thing. These wolf eels have approached divers in an aggressive manner that can be unnerving for someone not familiar with them. These wolf eels are still wild animals, despite their Muppet-like appearance.

Sea Lions

In the winter months, sea lions can be found in abundance at Race Rocks. The two types of sea lions found here are Steller (also called northern) and Californian. Stellers can grow to 3.5 metres (12 feet) in length and weigh up to 800 kilograms (2000 pounds). Californian sea lions are somewhat smaller but still weigh much more than a human.

Underwater, these massive mammals move like birds and are just as fast. Sea lions are wild animals and although they seem to be friendly and playful, their attitudes can change rapidly. They have been known to yank on fins, knock off the occasional mask, and even bite. With their size and speed, they must be respected.

If after reading the preceding paragraph you still want to dive with sea lions, here are a few recommendations.

- Enter the water away from the area where the sea lions are, then drift toward them under water.
- Make occasional eye contact but don't stare them down.
- Stay close to the bottom when they are near.
- Always move slowly and deliberately.
- Be mentally prepared to see them. If you are startled and you make a sudden movement toward them, they may consider your action threatening or aggressive.
- If you notice any aggressive behaviour—such as blowing bubbles into your face or continually "dive-bombing" you—move out of the area.

I must stress that sea lions are unpredictable wild animals and can be dangerous.

Elephant Seals

Elephant seals have been known to visit Race Rocks. Males commonly weigh over 2700 kilograms (6000 pounds) and they can grow to 6 metres in length (20 feet). Elephant seals can be much more aggressive than Steller or Californian sea lions.

Plankton

Plankton is the most basic element in the food chain. Every animal in the ocean—and, indirectly, every animal on land as well—relies on plankton to survive.

Phyto planktons are microscopic plants (algae) that use photosynthesis to grow, just like plants on land. The process of photosynthesis uses up carbon dioxide. Its waste product is oxygen. The phyto planktons of the world produce most of the earth's oxygen (more than 80 percent) and are in essence the basis of life on earth.

Zoo planktons are tiny animals, often in the first stages of their life. The smallest of these zoo plankton consume phyto plankton. The larger zoo plankton often eat other zoo plankton. Many of these zoo planktons are bioluminescent, which means at night they glow when they are agitated by diver movement. On your next night dive, turn your light off and wave your hand around and you will see the water glow.

Although both phyto and zoo planktons cause an overall reduction in underwater visibility, it is usually zoo planktons that we can see because they are larger.

Next time you are doing a safety stop, focus on the millions of tiny animals swimming all around you. Chances are you will be able to identify a few of these tiny creatures as miniatures of their adult counterparts.

Kelp

Certain species of kelp can grow up to 0.3 metres (1 foot) per day, which makes them the fastest growing thing on earth. The kelp around Victoria grows only in water that is 10 metres (30 feet) deep or shallower. Most people think that because they see kelp all year, it must grow all year long. In fact, when the daily amount of sunshine starts to decrease in the fall, the kelp starts to die. The roots of the kelp and the kelp itself are so strong that some dead kelp can last out the winter if it is not ripped up by the winter storms. The remains of the kelp that gets ripped up often clump together and float around for some time, which furthers the myth that kelp lives all year round.

For divers, kelp beds can be an incredible place to explore at the end of a dive when you are in the shallow water. They can also be a hazard if you are trying to make your way through a thick kelp bed. For the photographer, kelp with the sun shining through is a picture waiting to happen.

Current

Ocean currents are powerful forces that have a great impact on the sport of diving. Current can drift a diver by a dive site, giving you the feeling you are watching a movie passing by before you. That same current can create havoc for the unwary diver. The power that ocean currents hold over us as divers must be respected and understood. The better you understand current, the more you will learn to love it.

To learn what the currents are doing, get as many references as possible. The *Canadian Tide and Current Tables* are a basic necessity. The *Current Atlas* put out by the Canadian Hydrographic Service is also very good. If you buy the atlas, get *Murray's Tables* to go along with it.

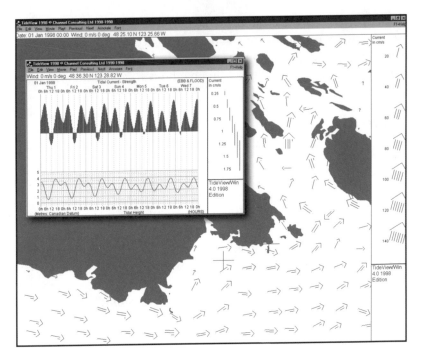

Sample Tideview *screen*

There is a computer program called *Tideview*, which presents an animated simulation of the currents in a given area. *Tideview* can show you a "movie" of current speed and direction in one-minute increments, as well as give tidal heights for any point that you click on (for more information about *Tideview*, check out http://www.channel.bc.ca/).

If you wish to learn more about tides and currents, there is a section at the beginning of the *Canadian Tide and Current Tables* that explains currents and how to use the tables. You may have to read it a few times to absorb some of the more technical information. There is also a "Definitions" section that contains important terms used throughout the tide tables.

Here are a few guidelines when predicting and assessing current:

- Rarely does the time of slack water coincide *exactly* with the time of high or low tide. This is important if you are predicting slack times using the tidal heights. It is most often better to predict current using the current tables.
- Arrive early so you can watch the current slow down and easily determine the direction.

- If the current has already slowed, watch the kelp or flotsam to determine the direction and speed of the current.
- Wind can affect the currents, so on windy days be aware that there may be some time difference between what the tables say and the reality out on the water.
- During a large tidal exchange or in a highly currented area you may have to get into the water before the current stops completely. If you time it right, the current will change direction while you are in the water and take you right back to your entry point.
- Be aware of the possibility of a back-eddy. A back-eddy occurs when a portion of the mainstream current diverges, curves around, and goes in the opposite direction to the mainstream current. This divergence usually occurs at a point or outcropping of land. When there is a back-eddy, the current will be moving opposite to what you would expect. The *Current Atlas* shows some of the larger back-eddies, but thousands of smaller ones are not shown in the atlas. Many of these smaller back-eddies are shown in *Tideview*.

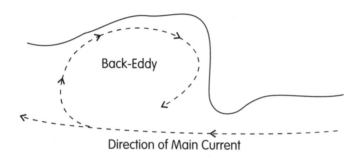

Direction of Main Current

- Dive with someone who has experience with the currents in the area.
- Dive on small tidal exchanges, especially where strong currents occur.
- Tide tables and charts are based on large areas and are not detailed enough to make predictions for some dive sites. You must evaluate the information and determine how it applies to a particular site. In the end, use the tidal information as a rough guide and evaluate what you see when you get to the site.

Throughout this book I will tell you as much as possible about the current at each dive site, but when you are about to enter the water it is your own accumulated knowledge and common sense that must guide you.

Underwater Visibility

Scuba diving is all about observing the underwater realm. How clearly a diver can observe anything depends on three main factors: plankton, suspended particles, and fresh water. All have varying effects on the clarity of the water. It is impossible to predict what the exact state of water clarity will be at any time. However, if you are aware of how the different factors affect the visibility or "vis," you may get a better idea of when and where to go diving.

An algae "bloom" occurs when the nutrient levels in the water rise and the sun shines constantly enough to spark the algae growth. Once the algae have bloomed, all the zoo plankton that feed on the algae bloom as well. The bloom is often heavier near the surface and usually hits its peak in about April or May. Generally, the winter months are the best time for good vis due to the lack of regular sunshine.

Suspended particles appear in the water as a result of stormy weather or freshwater run-off. Silt tends to build up on the rocks and kelp in areas that are not normally affected by the surge from waves. During a storm, the effects of the waves can be felt much deeper than normal. The larger the waves, the deeper the surge can be felt and the more silt is stirred up. As well, rivers pick up silt as they travel. When the river enters the ocean, the combination of silt and fresh water mixing with salt water can make for very poor visibility.

When fresh water mixes with salt water it creates a blurring effect. Since fresh water is lighter than salt water, it stays on top until mixed in by current or wind. Near river mouths there is a lot of mixing going on, and during the winter months, when rains are heavy, you are likely to find even more fresh water hanging around. If the rains are heavy enough you may find fresh water sitting on the surface everywhere, not just near river mouths. Luckily, since the fresh water sits on top, the blurring occurs only near the surface.

The **Saanich Inlet** deserves special mention concerning vis as it is unique in its patterns of visibility. (Some of the following does apply to other areas, but not to the same degree.) The inlet can have the best and the worst vis found in the Victoria area. Visibility of 50 metres (165 feet) is not unheard of, but neither is vis of 0.5 metres (1 or 2 feet). The plankton sometimes gets so thick that it blocks out all the sunlight, chokes itself out, and sinks to the bottom, creating incredible vis.

No matter what the visibility is in the inlet, there is often a "ceiling." A ceiling is a layer of water at the surface with poor vis. Because water in

the inlet does not circulate as much as it does in other areas, the top layer of water is generally warmer in the summer and possibly a little cooler in the winter. This temperature differential promotes algae growth, since certain types of algae are more inclined to grow at the slightly warmer or cooler temperatures.

One final tip on visibility. If the water looks black or dark from the surface, the vis will be good. The greener the water looks, the worse the vis will be.

Metric or Standard?

It was difficult to decide whether to use metric or standard measurements in this book. Here is what I decided and why.

- Most gear bought in Canada comes from the United States and is in standard measure, not metric. For this reason I decided to use feet for all depths as they pertain to diving.
- Most sources give current speeds in knots and I left them that way.
- Distances are given in kilometres.
- All other measurements are given in metric, with the standard conversion in parentheses.

How To Use This Guide

If anything in the book, particularly on the maps, seems unclear, refer back to this page. It contains information about the organization and layout of the information.

Written Information

For each site I list the name and indicate whether it is a boat or a shore dive. Further information on the site is listed under seven categories.

Attractions: I describe what there is to see at the site.

Directions: Under this heading I give the land-based directions and perhaps some directions for the boater. If the site is a "Boat Dive," I will state which boat launch to use. (See "Boat Launches and Dive Stores.")

Where To Dive: This is where you find out where to get in the water, where to go once you are down there, and where to get out.

Current: I'll give information about the currents at the dive site.

Depths: This is what you need to know about maximum depth and other depth-related details.

Hazards: This covers hazards specific to a particular site. I will not list everyday hazards such as weather, boats, bull kelp, jellyfish, and the risk of running low on air unless they are particularly bad.

Other Considerations: This is where I'll pass on general information that doesn't fall under other headings.

Maps

The map on the next page shows the general layout of the maps for each dive site. An overview map at the beginning of each section locates the area's dives and boat launches, while maps for each dive indicate currents, points of interest, hazards, etc.

Although I have tried to make the maps throughout this book as precise as possible, I cannot guarantee they are 100 percent accurate. Use these maps as a general reference for diving purposes only. Do not use them for navigational purposes.

Remember that true north is different from magnetic north. Magnetic north is approximately 20 degrees to the east of true north for the area covered in this book and is constantly changing. As of this writing, and depending on the location, magnetic north is moving west at an average rate of six minutes per year (one minute is one sixtieth of a degree). All maps are drawn to true north, but all other directions given (in degrees or otherwise) are compass headings (magnetic).

The depths shown on the maps are an average of all tides throughout the year. This means that the height of the tide when you go diving could

Dive Site Name
Shore or Boat Dive

This is an example of the maps that are found throughout this book.

The objects that are shaded the same colour as the land but that have no outline represent "drying rocks."
(A drying rock is land that is underwater at high tide and exposed at low tide.)

Some of the underwater reefs are shaded, with the depth contours visible underneath as shown below.

The dashed line with the arrow indicates a good path to follow for the dive. Some lines will have an arrow at both ends, indicating that you can start at either end.

The kelp represents kelp beds, which may or may not be present depending on the season and Mother Nature.

0-40 ft.

40-80 ft.

Over 80 ft.

Current

The solid lines with the arrows represent current and are usually accompanied by an explanation.

The small square inside the Locator Map is there to show you where the site is.

Victoria Area

This Map Is Not To Be Used For Navigation.
Use only as a general guide for diving purposes.

be anywhere from five feet higher to five feet lower than the depths shown on the maps.

The location of the kelp shown on the maps is only an approximation.

Before You Dive

Before you dive, take a look at the Dive BC web site (http://dive.bc.ca). It contains valuable information for diving around B.C. such as visibility reports, wildlife sighting reports, an underwater photography page, as well as underwater videos. You can submit your own visibility and wildlife reports to the page and the information will be updated instantly. You can also submit your own photos or videos for display online (see the web site for submission details). The web site contains contact information for dive shops, charter operators, major equipment vendors, PADI, and many other diving-related products and services around British Columbia and beyond. Every month there will be a different underwater photograph that you can download and use as wallpaper for your computer. Many other aspects of the web site are regularly changing and new features are being developed, so check back often.

And most important: dive safely and have fun.

BOAT LAUNCHES
AND DIVE STORES

Section I—Victoria Area

1. **Esquimalt Anglers Association**—1101 Munro Street, Esquimalt. There is a double-wide ramp with a good pier on each side. This is a well-maintained boat launch.

2. **James Bay Anglers Association**—75 Dallas Road—(250) 389-9684. There were no docks at this boat launch any of the times that I launched here, and a few of those times the ramps were covered with kelp and flotsam, making it difficult to launch.

3. **Cattle Point**—2900 block of Beach Drive in Uplands Park. There are two ramps at Cattle Point, one at each end of the Cattle Point Loop. This is a free public boat launch with no docks and no services.

Section II—Race Rocks & Metchosin Area

1. **Pacific Lions Marina**—241 Becher Bay Road—(250) 642-3816. Although it is only open from May 1 to the end of September, Pacific Lions Marina has a good ramp and services.

   To get to Pacific Lions Marina from Victoria, go north on Douglas Street (Trans-Canada Highway) until you come to the Colwood exit (Island Highway). Take the Colwood exit and follow the Island Highway (which will turn into Sooke Road) for approximately 15 kilometres. Turn left on Gillespie Road and follow it until you come to a T intersection where you turn left. You will now be on East Sooke Road. Turn right on Becher Bay Road and follow it to Pacific Lions Marina, which will be on your left. As you are making your way, keep an eye out for signs indicating "East Sooke Park (Aylard Farm)" and you will know that you are on the right track. However, if you get to the parking lot for East Sooke Park, you have gone a little too far.

2. **Cheanuh Marina** (Becher Bay Indian Reserve)—4901 East Sooke Road—(250) 478-4880. There is a good launch here, with all the services.

   To get to Cheanuh Marina from Victoria, go north on Douglas Street (Trans-Canada Highway) until you come to the Colwood exit (Island Highway). Take the Colwood exit and follow the Island Highway (which will turn into Sooke Road) for approximately 4 to 5 kilometres. Turn left on Metchosin Road. Follow Metchosin Road for about 8 kilometres until you come to Happy Valley Road. Turn right. About 600 metres along you will find Rocky Point Road. Turn left there. After a little more than 5 kilometres on Rocky Point Road, watch for the turn into Pedder Bay Marina on your left. Cheanuh Marina is about 2 kilometres past Pedder Bay, on your left.

3. **Pedder Bay Marina**—925 Pedder Bay Drive—(250) 478-1771. This is an excellent facility catering mainly to fishing enthusiasts, but it does see its fair share of divers. The staff can give you up-to-the-minute weather reports for Race Rocks.

   To get to Pedder Bay Marina from Victoria, go north on Douglas Street (Trans-Canada Highway) until you come to the Colwood exit (Island Highway). Take the Colwood exit and follow the Island Highway (which will turn into Sooke Road) for approximately 4 to 5 kilometres. Turn left on Metchosin Road. Follow Metchosin Road for about 8 kilometres until you come to Happy Valley Road, where you turn right. About 600 metres along it you will find Rocky Point Road. Turn left there. After a little more than 5 kilometres on Rocky Point Road, watch for the turn into Pedder Bay Marina on your left. There is a big sign—you can't miss it.

Section III—Saanich Inlet

1. **Tsartlip Boat Launch**—At the west end of Stellys Cross Road in the South Saanich Indian Reserve. This is the most convenient launch for most of the spots in the Saanich Inlet. The dock is sometimes in disrepair but is always useable. There is a fee for using this launch.

   To get to the Tsartlip launch from Victoria, go north on Blanshard Street until you come to the Royal Oak exit. Take the exit and turn left onto Royal Oak Drive. Follow Royal Oak Drive for a couple of blocks and then turn right onto West Saanich Road. Follow West Saanich Road until you get into Brentwood Bay. Just as you are leaving Brentwood Bay you will come to Stellys Cross Road. Turn left onto it and follow Stellys Cross Road to where it ends in something resembling a T intersection. Go to the right and pull over. This is where you pay for the launch. Continue on straight for about 20 metres and then turn left.

2. **Mill Bay Boat Launch**—740 Handy Road—(250) 743-4112. There is a free boat launch here, as well as a $5 boat launch in the adjacent Mill Bay Marina. The free boat launch is better at low tides, and I don't see any reason to pay $5 for the marina's launch except in cases where the free launch is not steep enough.

   To get to Mill Bay boat launch from Victoria, go north on Douglas Street (Trans-Canada Highway) and follow it up and over the Malahat Drive. On your way down the Malahat you will see a sign that tells you to turn right for the Mill Bay Ferry. Turn right there. You will be on Deloume Road. Take the first right, which is Mill Bay Road. After a couple of blocks, turn left on Handy Road. It will take you right down to the free boat launch. The marina is on the right.

3. **Goldstream Boathouse**—3540 Trans-Canada Highway—(250) 478-4407. This boat launch is not conveniently located for most of the dives in the Saanich Inlet but is an alternative if the others are busy.

   To get to the Goldstream Boathouse from Victoria, go north on Douglas Street (Trans-Canada Highway) and keep going until you pass Goldstream Park on your right. Just past the park, on your right, you will see the sign for the Goldstream Boathouse. Turn right.

Section IV—Sidney Area

1. **Sidney Boat Launch**—9500 block of Lochside Drive (right beside the Anacortes Ferry). This launch tends to be busy on summer weekends, but it is the best launch for diving around Sidney.

   To get to the Sidney boat launch from Victoria, go north on Blanshard Street, which turns into the Pat Bay Highway (#17), until you get to the turn-off for the airport. Turn right and then make a quick left. You will be on Lochside Drive. Approximately 2 kilometres later you will see a small park (Tulista Park) and the Anacortes Ferry on your right. Back up! You missed the turn. The turn-off is to your right just before the park and it actually looks like the parking lot for the park. Once you are in the parking lot you will see a one-lane path that leads 50 metres to the boat launch.

2. **Van Isle Marina**—2320 Harbour Road in Sidney—(250) 656-1138. There is a single wide boat launch with a good dock. At the time of writing this launch was two to three dollars more than the competition.

   To get to Van Isle Marina from Victoria, go north on Blanshard Street, which turns into the Pat Bay Highway (#17). Continue on the highway through the traffic lights at Beacon Avenue (the town of Sidney's main street) and then take the next exit to your right onto McDonald Park Road. There are no traffic lights at this exit. Follow McDonald Park Road a short distance and then turn right onto Resthaven Drive. Drive a few blocks until you see Harbour Road on your left; turn onto it. Keep watching on your right for a big blue sign with white lettering declaring "Van Isle Marina." Note: As you are driving down Resthaven Drive you will see a parking lot with a big green sign that says "Tsehum Harbour." There are a lot of boats moored here, but this is not Van Isle Marina.

3. **Island View Beach**—This ramp is not maintained, there are no docks, and it is poor at low tides. There is really no reason to launch at this ramp unless it is a hot summer weekend, in which case the Sidney boat launch is likely to be busy and the Island View ramp might not be a bad idea.

   To get to Island View Beach from Victoria, go north on Blanshard Street, which turns into the Pat Bay Highway (#17). When you get to Island View Road, turn right. Follow Island View Road as it twists and turns until you get to the parking lot. You will see a ramp a little to your right.

Section V—Sansum Narrows

1. **Cowichan Bay Boat Launch**—1800 block of Cowichan Bay Road. This is the best launch to use for the southern Sansum Narrows area. It is not as close to the narrows as Cherry Point Marina, but it is a lot easier to get to, it is free, and it has a better ramp.

   To get to the Cowichan Bay boat launch from Victoria, go north on Douglas Street, which becomes the Island Highway (Trans-Canada Highway), until you get to Cowichan Bay Road. Turn right. Follow Cowichan Bay Road all the way down to the water and the small community of Cowichan Bay. The road follows the business frontage. Once you are past the buildings on the right you will see the boat launch parking lot on your right. Turn right into the parking lot and you are there.

2. **Cherry Point Marina**—Off Sutherland Drive in Cowichan Bay— (250) 748-0435. This launch is not as well maintained as the Cowichan Bay boat launch and there is a fee for using it, so despite the fact that Cherry Point is a little closer to the dive sites than the Cowichan Bay launch, I still prefer the Cowichan Bay launch.

   To get to the Cherry Point Marina from Victoria, go north on Douglas Street, which becomes the Island Highway (Trans-Canada Highway), until you get to Cowichan Bay Road. Turn right. Follow Cowichan Bay Road to Cherry Point Road and turn right. Follow Cherry Point Road as it curves around. At the point where the road makes a 90 degree right turn, look to your left and you will see Sutherland Drive. Turn left onto Sutherland and follow it down to the marina and boat launch.

3. **Maple Bay Boat Launch**—At the end of Maple Bay Road. Any of the times that I have been to the Maple Bay launch I have seen no signs indicating there is a fee to use the launch and nobody has been around to ask, so I guess it is free. There are no services and no dock at this launch.

   To get to the Maple Bay boat launch from Victoria, go north on Douglas Street, which turns into the Island Highway (Trans-Canada Highway), and don't stop until you get to Duncan. Keep in the right lane as you cross the bridge going into Duncan, and turn right on Trunk Road, a couple of blocks farther along. Follow the signs to stay on Trunk Road and eventually it will turn into Maple Bay Road. At the end of Maple Bay Road there are a couple of stop signs. Keep heading towards the water. When you hit the second stop sign, turn left and watch for the boat ramp on your right (Maple Bay isn't big).

Dive Stores

The following are the dive stores in the area covered by this book at the time of printing. This list will be updated in future printings. Please send announcements of new dive store openings to the author via e-mail (update@dive.bc.ca).

Greater Victoria area

1. **Frank Whites Dive Stores**
   1855 Blanshard Street, Victoria
   Phone: (250) 385-4713
   Fax: (250) 385-4723
   and
   D-2200 Keating Cross Road, Central Saanich
   Phone: (250) 652-3375

2. **Ocean Centre**
   800 Cloverdale Avenue, Victoria
   Phone: (250) 475-2202
   Toll Free: 1-800-414-2202

3. **Ogden Point Dive Centre**
   199 Dallas Road, Victoria
   Phone: (250) 380-9119
   Fax: (250) 385-9110
   Email: jmadro@tnet.net

Duncan Area

1. **Giant Stride Diving**
   60 Kenneth Street, Duncan
   Phone: (250) 748-8864
   Toll Free: 1-800-634-5507

2. **Waterworld Dive Shop**
   6701 Beaumont Avenue, Maple Bay
   Phone: (250) 746-0991

3. **Pacific Water Sports**
   (Scuba lessons & air fills only)
   Shawnigan Lake
   Phone: (250) 743-1699

TOP TEN SITES

Check out a few of my favourite dives around Victoria.

1. **Race Rocks-West Wall:** One dive at this site will tell you why it made number one on this list. This site is only accessible by "live boat"—a boat with a driver.
2. **North Cod Reef:** This reef is an underwater haven for marine life of all sizes, shapes, and colours.
3. **Ten Mile Point:** This is definitely the best shore dive around Victoria. There is a good possibility of seeing some unusual animals like king crabs, grunt sculpins, octopuses, and wolf eels, to name a few.
4. **South Bedford Island:** On my first dive at this site I saw two octopuses and a wolf eel, along with countless other interesting creatures. Pieces of the wreck of the *Swordfish* lie on a ledge at this boat dive.
5. **Octopus Point:** This sheer wall is covered in anemones and various other marine life. Spectacular!
6. **Swordfish Island:** An incredible life-covered tunnel passes through one end of this small island. You won't be disappointed.
7. **HMCS *MacKenzie*:** Divers come from all over to see this 110-metre (366 foot) vessel. Now, several years after her sinking, the marine life has taken a strong hold.
8. **Ogden Point (The Breakwater):** This is the easiest shore dive around Victoria, with the best display of marine life starting at around flag #2. The breakwater is popular with divers of all skill levels and is excellent for night dives.
9. **Graham's Wall:** A wall, covered with marine life, that is accessible most of the time.
10. **Strongtide Island:** As the name suggests, there is a strong current to feed the abundant marine life.

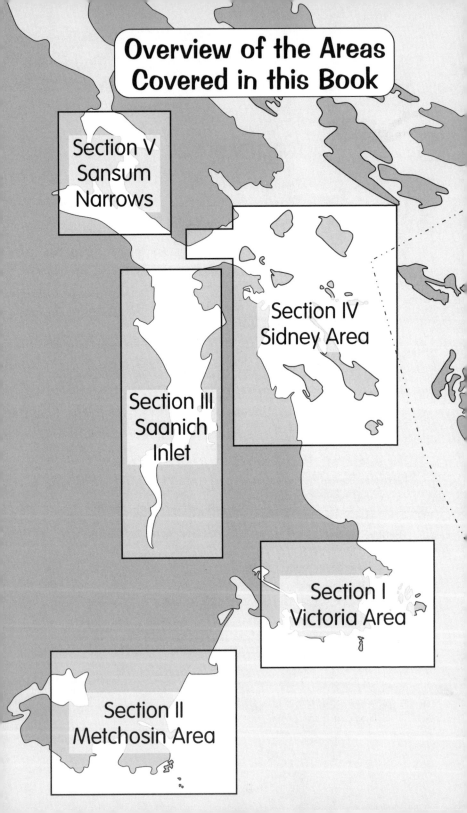

SECTION I

Victoria Area

The **Victoria** area has many great dive sites with convenient access that will appeal to divers of all skill levels. One of the most popular dive sites, Ogden Point (the Breakwater), is great for beginners, while one of the best shore dives that I have seen anywhere, Ten Mile Point, is a challenge for more advanced divers.

The Victoria waterfront is subject to more wind than most other places. It is exposed on three sides to fairly regular winds that can blow up quickly. Even light winds in this area seem to create large choppy waves, which can be uncomfortable if you're in a small boat or can make getting out of the water difficult on a shore dive. It is a good idea to head back to shore as soon as a wind starts to blow up rather than waiting until it gets strong.

Most of the dive sites around Victoria get quite busy in the summer, particularly Ogden Point, Spring Bay, and Ten Mile Point. Many divers like the convenience of diving close to the dive shops, which makes it quick and easy to get air fills, so these sites can get congested.

Shore Dives
Clover Point
Ogden Point (The Breakwater)
Saxe Point
Spring Bay
Ten Mile Point

Boat Dives
Brotchie Ledge
Discovery Island
Strongtide Island
Wreck of the *S.F. Tolmie*

Other Sites

Brinn Rock
Chain Islets
Esquimalt Lagoon
Fulford Reef
Mouat Reef
Telegraph Cove
Virtue Rock
Wreck of the *Green*

Victoria Area Overview

For more information about the boat launches see the "Boat Launches and Dive Stores" section in the beginning of this book.

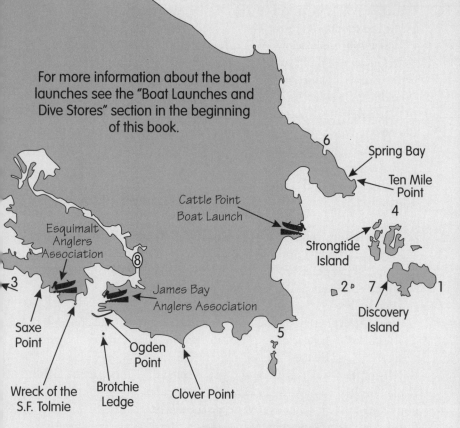

Spring Bay

Ten Mile Point

6

Cattle Point Boat Launch

Strongtide Island

4

Esquimalt Anglers Association

8

2

7

1

3

James Bay Anglers Association

Discovery Island

Saxe Point

Wreck of the S.F. Tolmie

Brotchie Ledge

Ogden Point

Clover Point

5

Boat Ramps

OTHER SITES

1. Brinn Rock
2. Chain Islets
3. Esquimalt Lagoon (not shown)
4. Fulford Reef
5. Mouat Reef
6. Telegraph Cove
7. Virtue Rock
8. Wreck of the Green

1) Esquimalt Anglers Association
   1101 Munro Street

2) James Bay Anglers Association
   75 Dallas Road
   Ph. 389-9684

3) Cattle Point Boat Launch
   2900 block of Beach Drive

Clover Point

Shore Dive

Attractions: A large kelp bed engulfs the eastern side of Clover Point during the summer months. The kelp bed is home to many creatures and is quite a sight from below, especially on a sunny day. Once you get past the kelp, you will find a lot of sea pens all along the sandy bottom, as well as many other invertebrates, crabs, and fish.

Directions: Go south on Douglas Street until it ends at a T intersection. Turn left onto Dallas Road. Follow Dallas Road for approximately 2 kilometres. When you get to the corner of Dallas Road and Moss Street, look to your right and you will see Clover Point.

Latitude—48° 24.2'

Longitude—123° 20.9'

Where To Dive: On the east side of Clover Point there is a building and a ramp that leads to the water. There is usually a good path through the kelp straight out from the ramp (though you should keep in mind that Mother Nature hasn't read this book). Once you have snorkelled through the kelp, submerge and go to the right (south). Follow the line where the rock meets the sand, as this is where there is the most to see. Turn around and exit back at the ramp.

Current: At the southern end of the point there are currents of up to 2 knots on large tidal exchanges. Dive any time on small tidal exchanges or at slack on large tidal exchanges. The current *almost* always goes seaward (south) on flood or ebb tides and gets stronger as you near the point. Remember you will usually be coming back against the current if you are not diving at slack, so budget your air appropriately.

Depths: It doesn't get much deeper than 40 feet unless you go out into the sand. The area where the rock and kelp meet the sand is about 30 feet deep and gets a little deeper the farther south you go.

Hazards: During the summer months the kelp can get extremely thick, and it can be tricky and sometimes dangerous to find a path through. There is a sewage outfall near Clover Point that extends approximately half a kilometre from shore. Some people don't like the idea of diving near this outfall even though it is a long way offshore. Heavy seas are a common hazard. Be aware that the current may get stronger as you near the point.

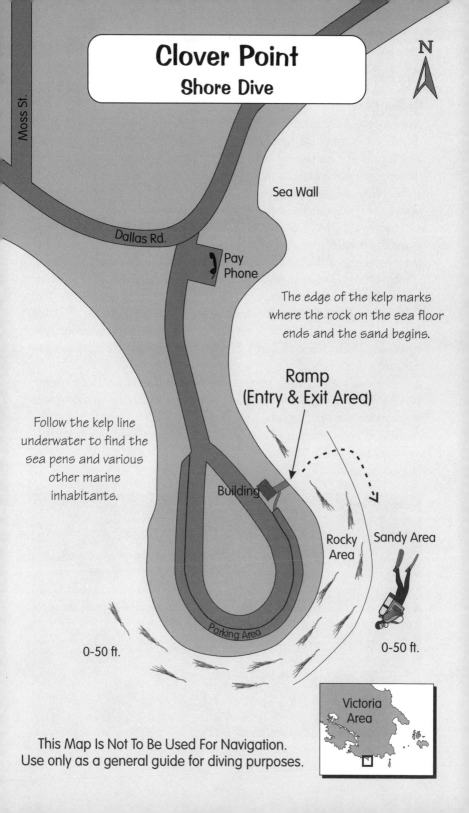

Ogden Point (The Breakwater)

Shore Dive

Attractions: Easy access for divers and minimal current along with a diversity of marine life have made Ogden Point a very popular dive site. The breakwater is made up of large rectangular stones. The gaps between these stones make ideal habitat for marine life large and small. For such an easy dive, Ogden Point has it all: lots of large fish, anemones galore, octopuses of various sizes, and even wolf eels.

Easy navigation and lots of "night-life" make Ogden Point a great place for diving after dark, too. The breakwater seems to have more than its share of nocturnal creatures including ratfish and octopuses.

In 1996 a dive shop and café were built at the breakwater, making it convenient to get air and lunch at the same place.

Directions: The Ogden Point breakwater is in the 100 block of Dallas Road. Go south on Douglas Street until it ends at a T intersection. Turn right onto Dallas Road and go 1.25 kilometres. Look to the left and you can't miss the breakwater.

There is parking right in front of the breakwater on Dallas Road. Just to the west of the breakwater there is a cheap pay parking area that is closer to the breakwater. If you plan to walk out along the breakwater, it is more convenient to park in the pay parking area.

Latitude-48° 24.8'

Longitude-123° 23.1'

Well-disguised decorator crab

Ogden Point
(The Breakwater)
Shore Dive

This dive site is a marine reserve. Spearfishing and collecting are prohibited.

The flags shown correspond to flags painted on the breakwater wall. Depths indicated are measured from the bottom of the breakwater, where the rock meets the sand.

#1
20 ft. deep

#2
40 ft. deep

#3
60 ft. deep

#4
70 ft. deep

#5
80 ft. deep

85 ft. deep

Light & Fog Signal

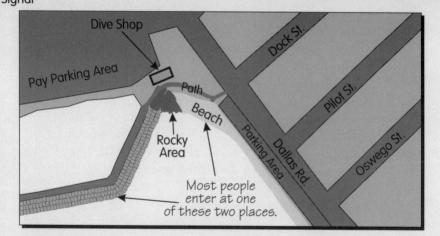

Dive Shop

Pay Parking Area

Path

Beach

Rocky Area

Dock St.

Pilot St.

Oswego St.

Parking Area

Dallas Rd.

Most people enter at one of these two places.

Below each dive flag, at a depth of approximately 25 feet, there are placards showing local marine life. These placards are often covered in algae and kelp, so look closely.

This Map Is Not To Be Used For Navigation. Use only as a general guide for diving purposes.

Victoria Area

Canary rockfish

Where To Dive: The Ogden Point breakwater is angled at two points. This creates three sections.

- The first section, up to the first corner, is shallow and there isn't much to see.
- The second section is the biggest section and the area that most divers explore.
- The third section is only for the hardy, unless you get there by boat.

There are many ways to approach your dive at the breakwater.

The easiest is to snorkel out to the first corner and go down there. Go out along the breakwater as far as your air dictates, then turn around and come back. As an alternative, you could walk out to the first corner instead of snorkelling.

A harder alternative is to walk as far as you can on the breakwater and then enter. Ideally you should get at least halfway between the first and second corners, or to the third flag marked on the breakwater. From there you just submerge and head back to shore.

The Ironman option is a 550-metre hike to the second corner or a 750-metre marathon to the end of the breakwater. If you have the energy, this is the best way to see the breakwater as there is no backtracking and you can start deeper and work shallower. It is unlikely that you will be able to make it from the end of the breakwater to shore on one tank of air, and if you do make it all the way back to shore, you will almost certainly miss a lot along the way. The advantage of going all the way to the end is that there is more to see there than closer in. If you have done the first two sections of the breakwater many times, walking out to the end will be like doing a new dive site. I have only done this horrendous hike twice, but I have dived at the end of the breakwater several times by boat, which is probably a better idea.

Current: The breakwater is a good spot to go anytime. The current isn't generally strong, but occasionally it flows in a seaward direction. This may be the result of tides alone, or sometimes the wind is a factor. The farther you go seaward, the stronger the current, especially once you get past the second corner. Remember to allow more time to get back if there is a seaward current (a current flowing away from shore). If you get low on air you can always walk back along the breakwater.

Depths: Maximum depth from the shore to the first corner is 20 feet. From the first corner to the second corner the range is from 20 to 80 feet deep. After the second corner it is 80 feet and deeper. No matter where you are on the breakwater, you can maintain a certain depth by following the "steps" or slope of the breakwater.

Hazards: Southerly winds, fishing line, and fishermen. Not so much a hazard as a drawback is the fact that there are lots of divers here. The good location and the gradually sloping bottom make this an ideal site for dive courses (mostly on weekends). As well, you either have to hike (or snorkel) a long way out before you dive or else go out and back along the same route, seeing everything twice.

Other Considerations: The breakwater is a marine sanctuary. Spearfishing and collecting are not permitted.

Saxe Point

Shore Dive

Attractions: This is an easy, shallow dive with limited but diverse invertebrate life.

Directions: From downtown Victoria go west on Pandora Street. Cross over the Johnson Street Bridge into Esquimalt. You will be on Esquimalt Road. Stay on this road for approximately 3 kilometres to Fraser Street on your left. Turn left on Fraser Street and follow it straight down to Saxe Point Park.

Latitude-48° 25.4'

Longitude-123° 25.1'

Where To Dive: To the northwest, or to your right, as you enter the parking lot is a trail that leads to the entry/exit point shown on the map.

Current: Current isn't a factor at this site except on the larger tidal exchanges. Even then it is often still "diveable." I have dived at Saxe Point during a large tidal exchange, getting in the water during full flood, and I didn't have too much trouble, although there may be times when it is not advisable.

Depths: If you dive following the contour of the land (as shown on the map), there is rock down to about 30 feet deep. Deeper than that it is sandy bottom.

Hazards: There is no protection from the waves when the wind picks up. One drawback is that, in the summer, leaf kelp covers the bottom and makes it very difficult to find anything.

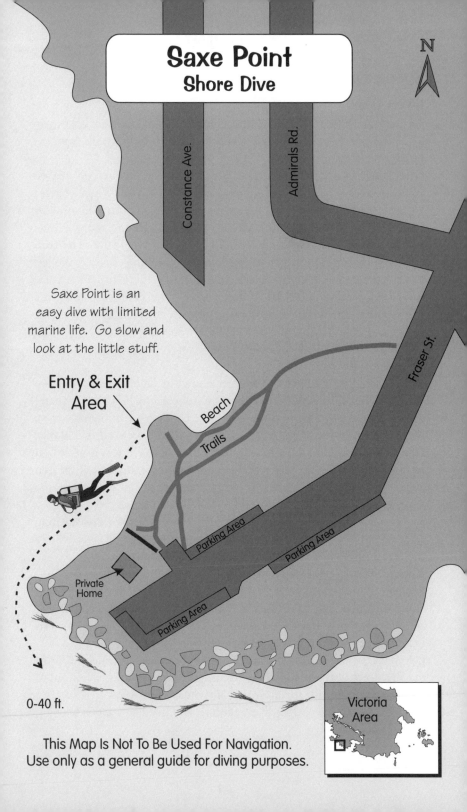

Saxe Point
Shore Dive

N

Constance Ave.

Admirals Rd.

Fraser St.

Saxe Point is an easy dive with limited marine life. Go slow and look at the little stuff.

Entry & Exit Area

Beach
Trails

Parking Area

Parking Area

Parking Area

Private Home

0-40 ft.

Victoria Area

This Map Is Not To Be Used For Navigation.
Use only as a general guide for diving purposes.

Spring Bay

Shore Dive

Attractions: Spring Bay is an easy dive, with easy access. There is a variety of underwater terrain and a fair variety of life in two directions from the beach.

Directions: To get to Spring Bay from downtown Victoria, go east on Hillside Avenue, which turns into Lansdowne Road. When you see Uplands Golf Course on your left, prepare to turn left onto Cadboro Bay Road. Follow Cadboro Bay Road for several kilometres and you will come to a four-way stop. Go straight through the four-way stop. The road curves to the right and then to the left. Just after the curve to the left watch for Seaview Road on your right and turn right. Once on Seaview Road take the first left onto Tudor Avenue. One kilometre along, the road turns to the left (it is still Tudor Avenue). At the end of Tudor the road narrows just before the parking lot for Spring Bay

Latitude-48° 27.4'

Longitude-123° 16.1'

Where To Dive: Straight out from the beach is sand and rock bottom with a few small reefs. Where the bottom is mostly rocky, closer to shore, there is a thick covering of leaf kelp. Under the kelp are numerous crabs, nudibranchs, and the like. As you go a little deeper, beyond the 30-foot range, the bottom becomes mostly sandy. East of the beach, nearing Ten Mile Point, there is another reef that is actually an extension of the Ten Mile Point wall (see the map). The closer you get to Ten Mile Point, the stronger the current is, but the amount of life increases as well.

To the north (left from the beach) there is a reef that extends a long way and is home to a variety of fish and invertebrates. This reef follows the shoreline, so it is not difficult to find or follow.

Current: Close to the beach at Spring Bay the current is basically non-existent at any point in the tidal fluctuation. The farther out you go in either direction, the more the currents will affect you, especially if you are going towards Ten Mile Point. Keep in mind that the current can increase in a hurry, so be careful how far you venture out.

Depth: Straight out from the beach the bottom slopes gradually. Out to the left (northeast), the top of the reef is quite shallow and the bottom of the reef varies, but for the most part is about 60 feet deep.

Hazards: Increasing current, bad visibility, and northerly winds blowing down Haro Strait.

Spring Bay
Shore Dive

N

The marine life becomes more concentrated the closer you get to Ten Mile Point.

Entry & Exit Area

The reef shown below is actually an extension of the Ten Mile Point wall.

Over 40 ft.

0-40 ft.

Beach

Parking Lot

Reef

Ten Mile Point

Spring Bay

Phyllis St.

Spring Bay Rd.

Medway St.

White Rock St.

Tudor Ave.

Baynes Rd.

Spring Bay is very popular with dive schools and divers in general. The parking lot can get quite full, especially on weekends.

Victoria Area

This Map Is Not To Be Used For Navigation. Use only as a general guide for diving purposes.

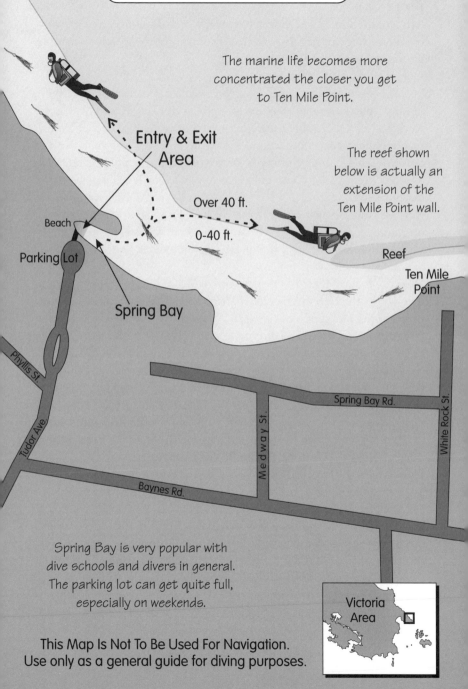

Ten Mile Point

Shore Dive

Attractions: Ten Mile Point is one of the best dives around Victoria—even though it's a shore dive. There is enough life to keep any diver happy for many a dive. Don't go too fast, take a light to explore every crack, and look at all the small creatures inhabiting the wall.

The beautiful, living wall of invertebrate life is an awesome spectacle. Plumose anemones cover most of the vertical areas of the wall, with every crack and space filled by some other form of marine life. Lots of animals that are rarely seen in other spots are common here. Grunt sculpins and red Irish lords (a couple of my favourites) make frequent appearances. If you are taking your camera, put on the macro lens. You won't be disappointed!

Ten Mile Point is a good place to find octopuses. There are plenty of den sites at the base of the wall and lots of octopus food in the surrounding area. Smaller octopuses can sometimes be found clinging to the face of the wall.

Directions: Ten Mile Point is at the end of White Rock Street in Cadboro Bay. To get there from downtown Victoria, go east on Hillside Avenue, which turns into Lansdowne Road. After you've passed Uplands Golf Course on your left, turn left onto Cadboro Bay Road. Follow Cadboro Bay Road for several kilometres and you will come to a four-way stop. Go straight through the four-way stop and follow the road as it curves to the right and then to the left. Just after the curve to the left watch for Seaview Road on your right and turn right. Once on Seaview Road, take the first left onto Tudor Avenue. After 1 kilometre the road turns to the left, but it is still Tudor Avenue. Continue on Tudor until you see Baynes Road on the right. Turn right onto Baynes Road, carry on to White Rock Street where you turn left, then go to the end and you're there.

Latitude-48° 27.4'

Longitude-123° 15.9'

Where To Dive: From a vantage point in the parking lot looking seaward, the best place to enter is slightly to the left, since the current most commonly flows from left to right. If the current is running in its usual direction it will probably take you around the corner to a small bay, which is the best place to exit. If the current is weak you may be able to spend a lot of time on the wall right out in front of the parking lot (north), where the life is best. There is no reason to go around the point to the

Ten Mile Point
Shore Dive

N

The marine life at this dive site is very diverse and concentrated. Ten Mile Point is by far the best shore dive around.

Caution!
Very Strong Tidal Currents Occur Often At This Site

The solid line illustrates the direction of the current during most flood or ebb tides. Due to a back-eddy, the current is most often going in an easterly direction.

Spring Bay

Over 80 ft.

40-80 ft.

0-40 ft.

Wall

Most common direction of current

Entry Area

House

Parking Lot

Fence

House

House

Path

Possible Exit Area

House

Spring Bay Rd.

White Rock St.

This dive site is a marine reserve. Spearfishing and collecting are prohibited.

Victoria Area

This Map Is Not To Be Used For Navigation.
Use only as a general guide for diving purposes.

small bay, marked as "possible exit area" on the map, if the current is not forcing you to go there. The best place to be is right on the wall.

Current: Dive on slack, preferably on a small tidal exchange. On a large tidal exchange you may not get much of a slack at all. The current at this site *usually* flows in an easterly direction regardless of whether it is a flood or ebb tide.

Depths: The wall starts at about 30 to 40 feet and bottoms out at about 80 feet. Beyond the wall the bottom slopes gently deeper and is sandy, with rocks strewn about.

Hazards: The entry area is very rocky and steep, so use extreme caution getting down the rock slope and into the water. Beware of kelp in the shallow areas and especially around the corner (to your right as you look out from the parking lot). The current at this site is powerful. Respect it. The wind around the Victoria waterfront can be very strong and erratic, and since this site is at a point of land, it seems to get more than its share of choppy water when it is windy. Ten Mile Point is also a popular fishing spot; consequently there are a lot of hooks and line lying around.

Other Considerations: Ten Mile Point is a marine sanctuary. Collecting and spearfishing are prohibited.

Brotchie Ledge

Boat Dive

Attractions: The wreck of the *San Pedro* lies in shallow water just to the north of the marker at Brotchie Ledge. The *San Pedro*, 100 metres (330 feet) long and 12 metres (42 feet) wide, was built for $350,000 and launched in 1882. Nine years later the boat was wedged onto Brotchie Ledge, and as the tide went out its own weight ripped holes in its bottom. Several hours later the *San Pedro* sank. There were no casualties. Salvage companies attempted to refloat the wreck, without success. The ship was not totally submerged and created an eyesore, so a company was hired to deal with the problem, which meant blowing the wreck to bits and salvaging the pieces for scrap. What remains today is the bottom part of the ship's hull and an assortment of other bits and pieces. Cabezon, ling cod, black rockfish, kelp greenling, and rockfish, all larger than average, make the remains of the ship their home.

Many years ago, Brotchie Ledge served as a garbage dump for Victoria. Consequently there are lots of bottles and other artifacts strewn about. Most of the garbage is concentrated on the southwest side of the light beacon.

With the shipwreck, the garbage, and the marine life, this is a great spot.

Directions: Launch at the James Bay Anglers ramp or the Esquimalt Anglers ramp.

If you launch at the James Bay Anglers ramp, go south out of the Inner Harbour. The breakwater will be on your left. As you near the end of the breakwater, look to the southeast (left) and you will see the light on Brotchie Ledge.

If you launch at the Esquimalt Anglers Ramp, exit Fleming Bay and go east-southeast, to the left. Go past the mouth of the Inner Harbour and straight out to Brotchie Ledge. As soon as you get out of Fleming Bay you will be able to see the light on Brotchie Ledge

Latitude-48° 24.4'

Longitude-123° 23.2'

Where To Dive: The wreck lies 10 metres north of the marker. It runs almost exactly east to west and is right in the middle of the kelp bed. The heaviest concentration of garbage is along the southwest side of the light beacon.

Current: Although the currents are not the strongest around, they are unpredictable. For the most accurate predictions use the Victoria *Tide*

Tables as opposed to the Race Passage *Current* Tables. Give yourself a lot of time to sit out and enjoy nature while you watch the current slow down. During larger tidal exchanges, dive at slack water. With a live boat and a small tidal exchange you can dive any time as long as you are experienced with currents.

Depths: The main portion of the wreck is no deeper than 30 feet. The garbage pile and the remaining pieces of the wreck are deeper, approximately 70 feet.

Hazards: Thick kelp beds all around the wreck, wind, and waves.

Other Considerations: Brotchie Ledge is part of the marine sanctuary that encompasses Ogden Point. It is illegal to remove any fish or marine life. Please do not remove any artifacts from this or any other wreck site.

Giant Pacific octopus

↑ Ogden Point

Brotchie Ledge
Boat Dive

N

This dive site is a marine reserve. Spearfishing and collecting are prohibited.

Any wreck sunk for over three years in British Columbia waters is protected by law. Collection or salvage of any items is against the law.

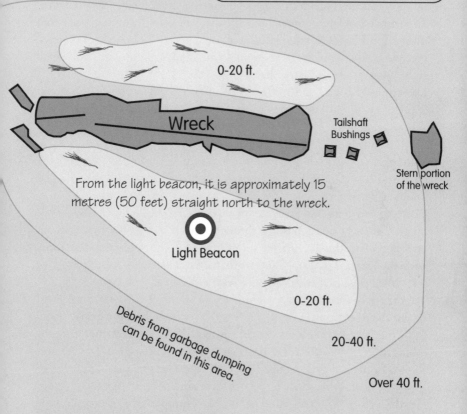

0-20 ft.

Wreck

Tailshaft Bushings

Stern portion of the wreck

From the light beacon, it is approximately 15 metres (50 feet) straight north to the wreck.

◉ Light Beacon

0-20 ft.

20-40 ft.

Debris from garbage dumping can be found in this area.

Over 40 ft.

Large fish can be found in great abundance at Brotchie Ledge, especially on the wreck.

This Map Is Not To Be Used For Navigation. Use only as a general guide for diving purposes.

Victoria Area

Discovery Island

Boat Dive

Attractions: A good wash of current sweeps by this reef, which juts out from the island about 150 metres. The fingernail-shaped reef forces the water to go around it and probably speeds it up enough to account for the diversity of life found on the reef's walls. There are spots from 100 to 120 feet where you'll find shallow caves and overhangs covered with plumose anemones. From 60 to 100 feet there is mostly smooth rock face with lots of larger invertebrate life that will keep the most experienced diver happy. In 60 feet and shallower you'll see an abundance of urchins, greenlings, ling cod, large anemones (other than plumose), kelp, small crabs, and smaller invertebrates.

Directions: Launch at the Cattle Point boat launch and go southeast approximately 3.5 kilometres to the west side of Discovery Island.

Latitude-48° 25.4'

Longitude-123° 15.1'

Where To Dive: Get into the water at whichever end of the reef the current dictates and follow it around. On the map you will see a dashed line that indicates a good dive path.

Current: Any hard and fast rule for this spot is out! Plumper Passage has up to 5-knot currents passing through, and it is possible that they go even faster past this site. Arrive a lot earlier than the predicted slack time, as this spot seems to change sooner than everywhere else does. Try to dive on a small tidal exchange and dive with a live boat.

One day a buddy and I entered the water at this site on a dead slack. Twenty minutes later there was a current going directly away from the island. This seaward current was pulling us off the reef into deeper water. We had a live boat, so when we surfaced the driver was able to come and pick us up. It is situations like this that demonstrate why you need a live boat at certain dive sites.

Depths: Where the reef runs parallel to Plumper Passage the bottom seems to flatten out at 100 to 120 feet. At either end of the reef, where it curves toward the shore, the bottom slopes shallower.

Hazards: Unpredictable current.

Other Considerations: Always use a live boat at this site.

Discovery Island
Boat Dive

N

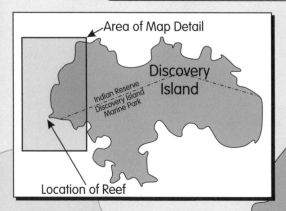

Area of Map Detail

Discovery Island

Indian Reserve
Discovery Island
Marine Park

Location of Reef

West Side of Discovery Island

This reef protrudes from the island and catches a lot of the 5-knot current that passes through Plumper Passage. This accounts for the diversity of marine life.

Caution!
Very Strong Tidal Currents Occur Often At This Site

The dashed line marks the best diving area. Start at whichever end the current dictates and follow the reef around.

Reef

Sloping Wall

0-30 ft.

30-60 ft.

60-80 ft.

80-100 ft.

Over 100 ft.

PLUMPER PASSAGE

Victoria Area

This Map Is Not To Be Used For Navigation.
Use only as a general guide for diving purposes.

Strongtide Island

Boat Dive

Attractions: The life is varied and plentiful at this site, but there are a few things that you are likely to remember because of their abundance. Large clumps of sulphur sponge are everywhere, as are giant barnacles, urchins, plumose anemones, and numerous other species.

Directions: Launch at Cattle Point. Strongtide Island is about 2.5 kilometres east-northeast of the Cattle Point boat launch. It is the northwesternmost of the Chatham Islands.

Latitude-48° 26.6'

Longitude-123° 15.2'

Where To Dive: The best part is at the northeastern tip, around the outside of the drying rock (see the map), but the whole northwest side of the island is good.

Current: Currents can run up to 6 knots on large tidal exchanges, so double-check your current calculations and don't be late.

Depths: Where the sloping area levels out to flat bottom, the depth is an average of 60 to 70 feet. At the northeast corner of the island it gets a little deeper.

Hazards: Strong current.

Other Considerations: The current picks up too fast to dive without a live boat.

BAYNES CHANNEL

Strongtide Island
Boat Dive

The current can move as fast as 6 knots through Baynes Channel.

Caution!
Very Strong Tidal Currents Occur Often At This Site

There is a lot of life along the whole northwest side of Strongtide Island, but the best part is at the northern end of the island.

Drying Rock

Over 100 ft.

80-100 ft.

The circle indicates the best diving area.

60-80 ft.

30-60 ft.

0-30 ft.

Strongtide Island

0-30 ft.

Victoria Area

This Map Is Not To Be Used For Navigation.
Use only as a general guide for diving purposes.

Wreck of the *S.F. Tolmie*

Boat Dive

Attractions: The wreck and the life calling it home are the main attractions at this site. For a long time this wreck was thought to be the *Major Tompkins*, but research by the Underwater Archaeological Society of British Columbia has proved it is the *S.F. Tolmie*, a wooden barge about 70 metres (240 feet) long. On the evening of December 27, 1944, the *S.F. Tolmie* was moored in Victoria Harbour. There were gale force winds that evening and the barge broke away from its moorings, dragged anchor, and landed on the rocks at Harrison Island.

The *S.F. Tolmie* was constructed mostly of wood, but all that remains today is the metal that held all the wood together. Although it appears as though the wreck is resting on its keel, it is actually lying on its side. The metal pieces sticking up from the sand are the "deck knees" that held the decks in place.

It is easy to see the impact that this wreck has had on the immediate area. It is home to an abundance of marine life, while the area around the wreck is relatively barren.

Red Irish lord

Wreck of the S. F. Tolmie
Boat Dive

N

The wreck of the S.F. Tolmie has for years been known erroneously to divers as the wreck of the Major Tompkins.

McLoughlin Point

Fleming Bay

Department of National Defense (DND) Property

Macaulay Point

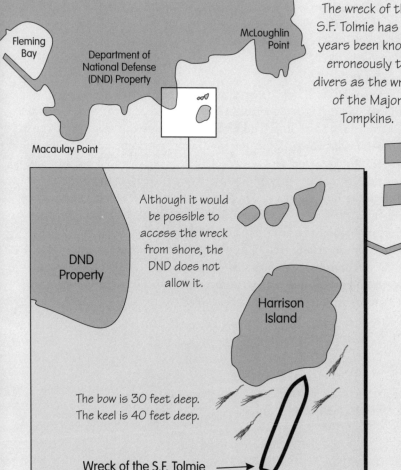

Although it would be possible to access the wreck from shore, the DND does not allow it.

DND Property

Harrison Island

Ogden Point

The bow is 30 feet deep.
The keel is 40 feet deep.

Wreck of the S.F. Tolmie ⟶

Any wreck sunk for over three years in British Columbia waters is protected by law. Collection or salvage of any items is against the law.

This Map Is Not To Be Used For Navigation.
Use only as a general guide for diving purposes.

Victoria Area

Directions: Launch from either the James Bay Anglers ramp or the Esquimalt Anglers ramp.

When you look out from the James Bay Anglers boat ramp you can see Harrison Island almost straight west across the harbour.

To get to Harrison Island from the Esquimalt Anglers ramp, go east (left) after departing Fleming Bay. Continue north (left) around Macaulay Point. Harrison Island will be on the left.

Latitude-48° 25.1'

Longitude-123° 24.1'

Where To Dive: There is an almost imperceptible point on the southeast side of Harrison Island. Go down at that point and continue south, following the line where the rock meets the sand. You can't miss the wreck, which lies in the sand almost straight north to south.

Current: This is a good spot to dive at any time in the tidal fluctuations. Large tidal exchanges may produce a weak current at this site.

Depths: The bow, which is the part closest to the island or pointing north, is in 30 feet of water; the stern is in about 40 feet.

Hazards: Victoria Harbour has a lot of boat traffic.

Other Considerations: This site used to be accessible from the shore, but the Department of National Defence (DND), which owns the property, now prohibits access from the beach. Please do not remove any artifacts from this or any other wreck site.

Other Sites

Shore Dives

To get to **Esquimalt Lagoon** from Victoria, follow the Trans-Canada Highway (#1) north to the Old Island Highway (#14). Take the Old Island Highway to Ocean Boulevard, on the left just past the Juan De Fuca Recreation Centre. Ocean Boulevard will take you right down the hill to Esquimalt Lagoon. Park just past the bridge. Dive just south of the bridge, outside the lagoon. Don't dive in the lagoon itself, as there is nothing to see there. This site is known as a place to catch crabs and is an easy place for a night dive. Large skates are not uncommon, especially near the beach. On one dive I thought the bottom was moving, only to discover it was a huge skate slowly moving away. The current is weak to non-existent.

Latitude-48° 25.7'
Longitude-123° 27.5'

Telegraph Cove is located in the Cadboro Bay area. To get there from downtown go east on Hillside Avenue, which turns into Lansdowne Road. When you've passed Uplands Golf Course on your left, turn left onto Cadboro Bay Road, continuing on it straight through the four-way stop. The road curves to the right and then to the left. Immediately after this you will come to another four-way stop. Go through this four-way stop as well. The road narrows and becomes Telegraph Bay

Clown nudibranch

Road, which you should follow straight down to the water. This is a shallow dive with limited life along the rocks on either side. Scuba instructors often use this site for their classes.

Latitude-48° 27.8'
Longitude-123° 16.7'

The **Wreck of the** *Green* can be found in the Inner Harbour (see the map on the next page). The *Green* was a 30-metre (102 feet), iron-hulled whaler. It was built in 1909 and sank April 4, 1966. The poor visibility and muddy bottom are the biggest drawbacks of this site. The wreck is the attraction here as there is little sea life on or around it. If you like wrecks it's worth at least one dive; otherwise there's not much point in diving this site. See the map for important details.

Latitude-48° 25.8'
Longitude-123° 22.2'

Giant (dancing) nudibranch

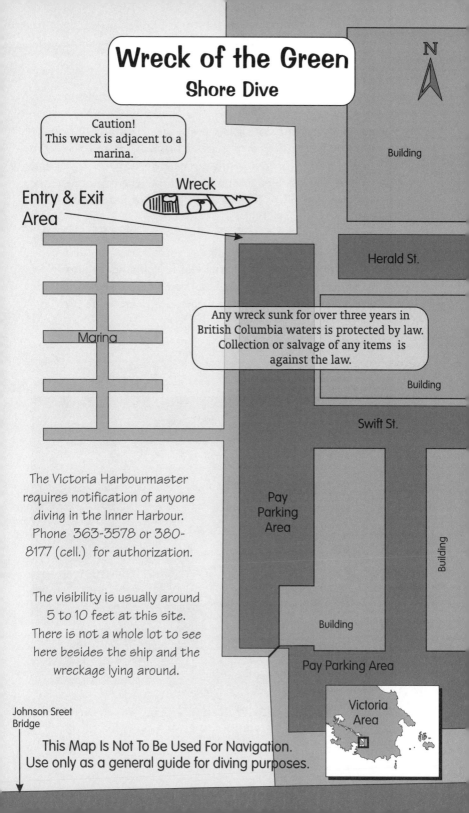

Boat Dives

Cattle Point is the closest place to launch for all of the following sites.

Brinn Rock is on the east side of Discovery Island, directly in front of the lighthouse. For the best dive, start at Brinn Rock and go to the southeast. The bottom slopes gently deeper, with lots of rocks and reefs to explore. There are concentrations of different types of marine life as you move along. It is best to dive this site with a live boat.

Latitude-48° 25.5'
Longitude-123° 13.2'

The **Chain Islets** are southeast of the Cattle Point boat ramps. The islets provide areas where you can hide from the current or at least find an area with less current. There is plentiful marine life with lots of octopuses.

Latitude-48° 25.3'
Longitude-123° 16.0'

Tiger rockfish

Fulford Reef is at the eastern entrance to Baynes Channel, at the northeast end of the Chatham Islands. The best area to dive is on the northeast side of the reef. From the marker, dive to the southeast. Dive at slack tide.

Latitude-48° 26.8'
Longitude-123° 14.4'

Mouat Reef is between the northern tip of Trial Island and Gonzales Point. Dive just south of the marker. The current flows at up to 3 knots, so dive with a live boat at slack tide.

Latitude-48° 24.5'
Longitude-123° 17.9'

Virtue Rock is at the south end of Plumper Passage between the Chain Islets and Discovery Island. There are lots of kelp, fish, and invertebrates here, with the most life at the north end of the reef. Dive at slack with a live boat.

Latitude-48° 25.1'
Longitude-123° 15.2'

Giant Pacific octopus

SECTION II

Race Rocks & Metchosin Area

I have gone diving all around the world, but I have never found a diving experience quite like the one in the **Metchosin** area, especially at Race Rocks. This locale often gets better visibility than any of the others covered in this book. Couple the good visibility with incredible marine life (including sea lions) and you have some world-class diving. There were many times I would lie in the boat between dives and think how lucky I was to be there and to do the diving that I was doing.

The one drawback is that the Metchosin area dive sites are hard to get to. For one thing, all of them are boat dives. When you add in other factors such as the distance from Victoria, the region's inclement weather, and wicked currents, these sites are out of bounds for a lot of divers. Despite the difficulty in getting to them, however, this area is my first choice when I go diving. If you have never been out to Metchosin, I suggest that you get out on a dive charter and experience the area that way first, even if you do own a boat. Once you have gained some experience with the currents and the sites of the area, you will be more confident to go out on your own with friends. Keep in mind that unless you are diving at Swordfish Island or the wreck of the *Barnard Castle* you will need a boat and driver (live boat) for the sites in this area.

Boat Dives
Beechey Head
Race Rocks
South Bedford Island (Wreck of the *Swordfish*)
Swordfish Island
Wreck of the *Barnard Castle*

Metchosin Area Overview

For more information about the boat launches
see the "Boat Launches and Dive Stores"
section in the beginning of this book.

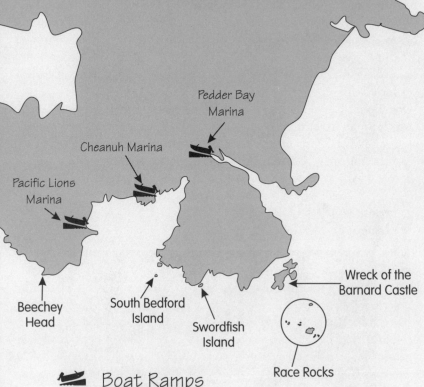

Pedder Bay
Marina

Cheanuh Marina

Pacific Lions
Marina

Beechey
Head

South Bedford
Island

Swordfish
Island

Wreck of the
Barnard Castle

Race Rocks

Boat Ramps

1) Pacific Lions Marina
    241 Becher Bay Road
    Ph. 642-3816
    (Only open from May 1 to the end of September)
2) Cheanuh Marina
    4901 East Sooke Road
    Ph. 478-4880
3) Pedder Bay Marina
    925 Pedder Bay Drive
    Ph. 478-1771

Beechey Head

Boat Dive

Attractions: An abundance of invertebrates as well as a large population of fish make this an incredible dive site. Just about every type of sponge found in the area is present here. Nudibranchs, starfish, and crabs that are rarely seen elsewhere make frequent appearances. Soft corals can be found on the wall at the west side of the reef. Large schools of black rockfish dominate the area. Kelp greenlings and ling cod also show themselves in large numbers, and there are occasional sightings of china rockfish. In the shallow water you can sometimes see enormous schools of small fish, with various larger fish, including salmon, darting in for a feast.

Directions: The closest place to launch is at the Pacific Lions Marina, which is only open from May 1 to the end of September. When Pacific Lions Marina is not open, Cheanuh Marina is the next closest boat launch. You may be better off to get on a charter out of Victoria or Sooke. That way all you have to do is dive and not worry about getting there.

Latitude-48° 18.8'
Longitude-123° 39.2'

Hermit crab

Beechey Head
Boat Dive

Be aware of a back-eddy that may occur in this bay on an ebb tide. This back-eddy creates a current that travels in a seaward direction, as indicated by the arrows.

East Sooke Park

Trail

Beechey Head

Wall

Reef

0-30 ft.

30-60 ft.

60-100 ft.

The reef marks the area where the life is the most concentrated. The best part of the dive starts at around 50 feet deep and continues into the depths.

Over 100 ft.

General direction of ebb current

Metchosin Area

This Map Is Not To Be Used For Navigation.
Use only as a general guide for diving purposes.

Where to Dive: The best and most concentrated life is straight out from the point. Start on either side of the point and follow it around. On the west side there is a wall, from 30 to 80 feet deep, extending out about 100 feet.

Current: The current is wicked at the best of times. Dive on slack, preferably on a small tidal exchange. Ebb tides commonly produce a back-eddy in the bay to the west of the point. This back-eddy can create a seaward current on both sides of the point.

Use the Race Rocks current predictions and arrive a little earlier than the time they give, as the tide seems to change sooner at Beechey Head. (Race Rocks Current Tables are on pages 62 to 65 of the *Canadian Tide and Current Tables.*)

Depths: The top of the reef ranges from 30 to 60 feet. The base of the reef is 60 feet and deeper.

Hazards: This is a popular spot for fishing, from the shore and by boat, and it is not unusual to see an angler's cannonball drift by. The wind and current are formidable obstacles at this site, and between the two of them it can be difficult to find a time to dive at this site; be sure to respect both.

Other Considerations: Always dive with a live boat and tow a float, as it can be difficult for your driver to follow your bubbles. As long as your driver knows exactly where you are, he can fend off anyone who is out fishing.

Race Rocks

Boat Dive

Attractions: The attraction here is life, large and small, abundant and incredible. On one dive my buddy and I were sailing along in the current when I spotted a wolf eel. We stopped to look at the wolf eel but were sidetracked by the octopus that we almost landed on. Everywhere you look at Race Rocks you will find life in some form. Some places are so thick with invertebrates that you can't see the rocks, but concentrations do vary. Steeper areas seem to be better. The numerous fish seem to be larger here than in other areas. Seals are plentiful all year round and if you are lucky, a pod of killer whales may make an appearance at the surface. Octopuses and wolf eels are common sights, but you may not spot them if you are too busy watching Race Rock's main attraction, for me at least, the sea lions. In the winter months sea lions cover almost every rock except Great Race. They are a big attraction for sightseers and divers alike and provide hours of

Basket star surrounded by sponges and anemones

entertainment above and below the water. Race Rocks is such a large area and there is so much life that you could dive here hundreds of times and never get bored.

Directions: Launch at Pedder Bay Marina and go south, keeping to the right (west) side of the inlet. As you approach the mouth of the inlet, watch for the lighthouse and Race Rocks. You may be better off to get on a charter out of Victoria or Sooke. That way all you have to do is dive and not worry about getting out here.

    Latitude-48° 18'

    Longitude-123° 32.2'

Where To Dive: There are many possible entry and exit points at Race Rocks. There are some areas around Rosedale Rock (the pinnacles shown on the map) that have plentiful and diverse life. My favourite spot is the West Race Rock wall (as shown on the map). It has just about everything that a person can see at Race Rocks. On the north side is a wall with "No Vacancy" (it's absolutely covered), and if you dive there in the winter you are bound to be greeted by at least a few sea lions.

Race Rocks is a great place to explore and I have laid out some possible routes to follow on the maps. Many ships have crashed on the shores of Race Rocks, so it is not uncommon to find artifacts or even pieces of wrecks. Just south of West Race Rock I found a large anchor on a small reef at about 55 feet deep. I have also found lots of other smaller things by drifting into new places, so keep your eyes open and you are likely to see some treasures.

If you are out to encounter sea lions, stay in the shallow areas of West, Central, and North Race Rocks. If it is seals you want to see, Great Race Rock is the place to be. Great Race is also a good place to go if the current is picking up. Hide on the side opposite the direction of the current.

Current: There are several reasons the current at Race Rocks is as strong as it is so much of the time. The Strait of Juan de Fuca narrows at Race Rocks, so the huge volume of water passing through the Strait is forced to run through a smaller area. Consequently it must go faster. Race Rocks is also much shallower than the surrounding area, and the same rule applies: the same volume of water must pass over (or go around) a shallower area. Yet another reason for this constant current is that a back-eddy often forms in Parry Bay (northeast of Race Rocks) just before slack on a flood tide. Although the current can be treacherous

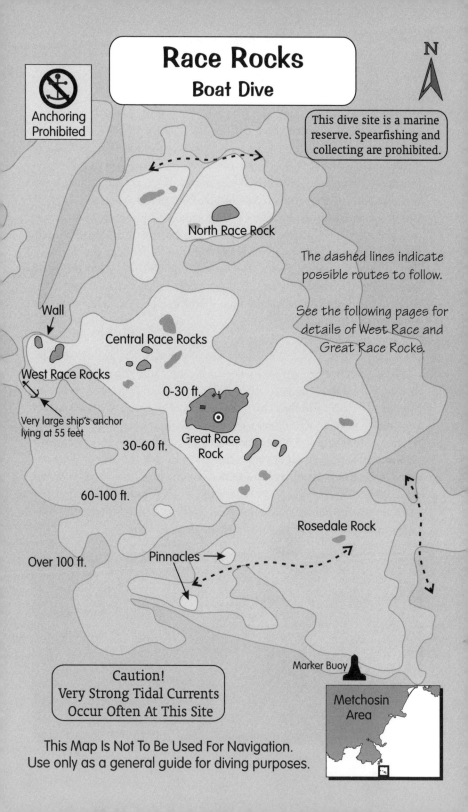

Race Rocks
Boat Dive

N

Anchoring Prohibited

This dive site is a marine reserve. Spearfishing and collecting are prohibited.

North Race Rock

The dashed lines indicate possible routes to follow.

See the following pages for details of West Race and Great Race Rocks.

Wall

Central Race Rocks

West Race Rocks

Very large ship's anchor lying at 55 feet

0-30 ft.

Great Race Rock

30-60 ft.

60-100 ft.

Rosedale Rock

Over 100 ft.

Pinnacles →

Marker Buoy

Caution!
Very Strong Tidal Currents
Occur Often At This Site

Metchosin Area

This Map Is Not To Be Used For Navigation.
Use only as a general guide for diving purposes.

for divers, it also brings the life-giving nutrients that make Race Rocks the incredible haven for marine life that it is.

Always dive on slack (or what there is of a slack). If there is a period in the day when there is a small exchange in the tide, dive on the slack that follows the small exchange. Use the Race Rocks Current Tables on pages 62 to 65 of the *Canadian Tide and Current Tables*.

Hazards: Strong and unpredictable current, rough seas, kelp, sea lions, boaters, and great white sharks (just kidding about that last one).

Other Considerations: Race Rocks is an ecological preserve. Spearfishing or collecting anything is prohibited. Anchoring is also prohibited. Please be careful not to disturb the wildlife, especially the sea lions that are on the rocks. Enter the water a fair distance from the rocks and advise the driver not to go near them. If you surface near the rocks, it is good practice for the boat driver to stay away and for you to swim to the boat.

Any ship sunk for over three years in British Columbia waters is protected by law. Collection or salvage of any items is against the law.

Since anchoring is illegal, the only way (and the safest way) to dive at Race Rocks is with a live boat. You should also tow a surface float or dive flag to make it easy for the driver to track you. During the course of a dive at Race Rocks the current could take you a long way. If you are not using a float, the boat may be looking for you in the wrong place when you surface, leaving you adrift for a long time. (Does it sound like that comment came from experience?) Having your driver follow divers' bubbles isn't a reliable method for a few reasons: sea lions often blow bubbles, current can whisk the bubbles away, and rough water can make them hard to spot.

Sea lions

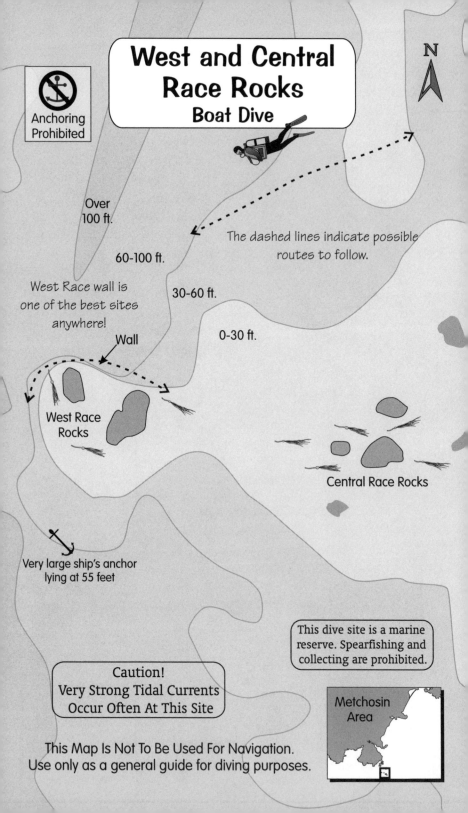

West and Central Race Rocks
Boat Dive

N

Anchoring Prohibited

Over 100 ft.

The dashed lines indicate possible routes to follow.

60-100 ft.

West Race wall is one of the best sites anywhere!

30-60 ft.

0-30 ft.

Wall

West Race Rocks

Central Race Rocks

Very large ship's anchor lying at 55 feet

This dive site is a marine reserve. Spearfishing and collecting are prohibited.

Caution!
Very Strong Tidal Currents
Occur Often At This Site

Metchosin Area

This Map Is Not To Be Used For Navigation.
Use only as a general guide for diving purposes.

Great Race
Boat Dive

Around Great Race Rock there are excellent places to dive that are hidden from the current. Which side you choose to hide on depends on whether the tide is ebbing or flooding.

The dashed lines indicate possible routes to follow.

Great
Race
Rock

Lighthouse

This route is all but impassable in the summer months due to very thick kelp.

0-40 ft.

40-70 ft.

This dive site is a marine reserve. Spearfishing and collecting are prohibited.

Caution!
Very Strong Tidal Currents
Occur Often At This Site

Metchosin
Area

This Map Is Not To Be Used For Navigation.
Use only as a general guide for diving purposes.

South Bedford Island (Wreck of the *Swordfish*)

Boat Dive

Attractions: On the southeast side of the island there is a steep wall that is covered with life. Where the plumose anemones are not covering the wall, many other forms of marine life have taken hold. Schools of black cod, cabezon, octopuses (I saw two clinging to the wall on one dive), grunt sculpins, basket stars, and every kind of anemone are a few of the things that you could expect to see.

Wreckage from the *Swordfish* lies at the southeast side of this little island. The wreck was originally believed to have been at what is now called Swordfish Island. It was later determined that the ship actually sank at South Bedford Island. The wreck isn't a big thrill, but don't fret; the marine life will more than occupy your time if battling the current does not.

Directions: The closest place to launch is at the Pacific Lions Marina, which is only open from May 1 to the end of September. Cheanuh Marina has the next closest boat launch. You may be better off to get on a charter out of Victoria or Sooke. That way all you have to do is dive and not worry about getting there.

Latitude-48° 18.7'

Longitude-123° 36.2'

Where To Dive: When you first arrive at this little island, make sure that you drive around it a few times and refer to the map to get your bearings. It looks easy enough on the map, but when you get there it is hard to discern the corners of the island. The south and southeast sides of the island look like one continuous side, but if you look closer you will notice a little point and a change of angle. The best route to follow is shown on the map. This route leads you along the wall, which usually consumes the whole dive. Take your time, there is lots to miss if you go too fast.

You can see parts of the wreck of the *Swordfish* on a shallow shelf on the southeast side of the island, while other parts have been swept off the shelf and into deeper water.

Current: One time we pushed the tide tables a little too far and it felt like an alien creature was trying to rip my body apart in every direction. The current swirls, tumbles, and back-eddies around South Bedford, so make sure to dive on slack. Go for a small tidal exchange if possible and arrive early to assess the currents. Due to a back-eddy, the current sometimes flows in an easterly (flood) direction during an ebb tide, and it can be going many different directions depending on where you are at any particular time. It is common to feel current going up (updraft) or down (downdraft). I highly recommend you have a live boat when diving this site. The current picks up so fast that you could be whisked past where your boat is anchored, with no hope of swimming back to it. Use the Race Rocks Current Tables on pages 62 to 65 of the *Canadian Tide and Current Tables*.

Depths: The wall starts at around 30 feet and flattens out at around 100 feet deep.

Hazards: Rough seas and current can be daunting at this site.

Other Considerations: Use a live boat to dive at this site.

Octopus shooting ink

South Bedford Island
Boat Dive

N

West
Bedford
Island

Vancouver Island

Large
Bedford
Island

South Bedford
Island

Church
Point

Swordfish
Island

The arrow above indicates the most common
direction of current. The current flows in an
easterly direction on flood tides, as well as some
ebb tides, due to a back-eddy.

Church
Island

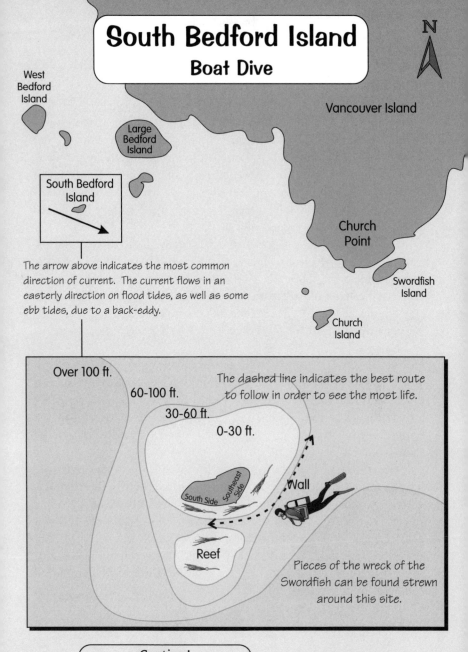

Over 100 ft.

60-100 ft.

The dashed line indicates the best route
to follow in order to see the most life.

30-60 ft.

0-30 ft.

Southeast
Side

South Side

Wall

Reef

Pieces of the wreck of the
Swordfish can be found strewn
around this site.

Caution!
Very Strong Tidal Currents
Occur Often At This Site

This Map Is Not To Be Used For Navigation.
Use only as a general guide for diving purposes.

Metchosin
Area

Swordfish Island

Boat Dive

Attractions: A tunnel runs through one end of this small island. The walls and ceiling of this tunnel are covered by a diverse collection of invertebrates, including soft corals. The life outside the tunnel is not nearly as plentiful, but there are often seals swimming about and there are a lot of greenlings that have become very tame. Another big attraction of this site is the fact that you can dive it just about any time. It is a great second dive to do after Race Rocks when the current has picked up too much to do a second dive at the Race.

Directions: The closest place to launch is at the Pacific Lions Marina, which is only open from May 1 to the end of September. If Pacific Lions is not open, Cheanuh Marina has the next closest boat launch. You may be better off to get on a charter out of Victoria or Sooke. That way all you have to do is dive and not worry about getting here.

Latitude-48° 18.6'

Longitude-123° 34.9'

Where To Dive: I usually start at the northeast end of the island, where I go to my maximum depth (60-80 feet) and follow the contour of the island to the southeast end. Then I turn around and start going a little shallower until I get back closer to the northeast end of the island, where I finish up in the tunnel (see the dashed line on the map).

The tunnel is about 15 feet deep. It can be hard to find, especially in the summer when there is an abundance of kelp hiding the entrance. The most reliable way to find it is to surface and locate the little "niche" in the rock (see the map) and then follow it down. You will have to fight your way through the kelp to get to the entrance. You can go in from the other side, but it is even harder to find the entrance from that direction. If you plan on entering the tunnel, here are a couple of things to keep in mind:

- It can be dangerous to go into overhead environments such as caves, tunnels, or wrecks. Do not enter unless you are properly trained.

- You must have perfect buoyancy control to avoid harming the delicate life in this narrow tunnel. Remember that the tunnel is shallow. If you are a little light on the weight belt, don't go in and bounce off the ceiling.

Swordfish Island
Boat Dive

Side View (from southeast side)

Gap in the rock

The tunnel is below the gap in the rock at a depth of 15 feet.

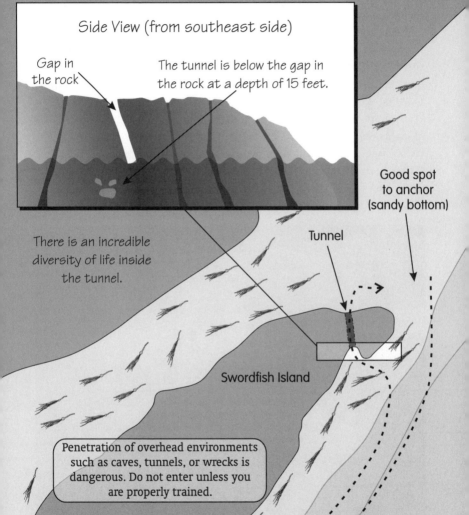

Good spot to anchor (sandy bottom)

Tunnel

There is an incredible diversity of life inside the tunnel.

Swordfish Island

Penetration of overhead environments such as caves, tunnels, or wrecks is dangerous. Do not enter unless you are properly trained.

0-30 ft.

30-80 ft.

Over 80 ft.

This Map Is Not To Be Used For Navigation.
Use only as a general guide for diving purposes.

Metchosin Area

Current: This is a good spot for a second dive after Race Rocks or South Bedford Island. When the current is too strong at those sites, you can almost always dive at Swordfish Island. On a large tidal exchange the current can be a factor but is not usually strong enough to keep you out of the water. The current inside the tunnel can be stronger than the surrounding current so be careful—for yourself and also for the delicate invertebrates on the tunnel wall and ceiling. You don't want to bash them as the current carries you through the tunnel.

Depths: The southeast side of the island goes from rocky slope to sandy bottom at about 70 to 80 feet deep.

Hazards: Kelp and rough seas while returning to the boat launch. The vis is often not as good here as it is in other nearby areas.

Other Considerations: You can anchor right off the northeast end of the island where the bottom is only about 30 to 40 feet deep.

Kelp greenling

Wreck of the *Barnard Castle*

Boat Dive

Attractions: The *Barnard Castle* was a 79-metre (260 foot) coal-carrying steamer. In 1886 it hit Rosedale Reef and managed to make it to Pilot Bay on Bentinck Island before it sank. In 1992 the Underwater Archaeological Society of British Columbia (UASBC) completed an underwater interpretive trail around the wreck. This trail is made up of eight plaques in various locations around the ship. Each plaque carries a description of the particular artifact to be found at that location on the wreck, along with a map of the site showing your current position. Although the wreck is over a hundred years old, there is still a lot to see. The boilers alone are quite impressive. Most of the bow of

Hanging out

the wreck has disintegrated, but there is a lot of the stern left. There are some large pieces of coal and various artifacts lying around. It is well worth at least one look.

Directions: Launch at Pedder Bay Marina and go south, keeping to the right (west) side of the inlet. As you approach the mouth of the inlet, look to your right and you will see Bentinck Island. The wreck lies in Pilot Bay on the south side of the island. There is a small white moorage buoy in the middle of the bay. It is usually attached to some barrels on the port side of the wreck, although from time to time the buoy does disappear—and then it takes some time for it to be replaced. If the buoy is missing when you arrive here, just use the map as a reference, swim across the bay, and you should be able to find the wreck without too much trouble.

Latitude-48° 18.7'

Longitude-123° 32.4'

Where To Dive: Just follow the buoy line down to the bottom, then go east about 4.5 metres (15 feet) and you will run into the wreck. The plaques, which are placed around the wreck, are relatively easy to find but always require cleaning to be read.

Current: On large tidal exchanges the current can be up to 2 knots on the stern (southern) part of the wreck. Around the rest of the wreck it is almost always less than a knot. The bay offers more protection from the current during flood tides than ebb tides, so the best time to dive is at slack or during a flood tide. Use the Race Rocks Current Tables on pages 62 to 65 of the *Canadian Tide and Current Tables*.

Depths: Most of the stern portion is in about 40 feet of water while most of the bow wreckage lies in 30 feet or less.

Hazards: Sharp wreckage and getting entangled in the wreckage are the two biggest hazards.

Other Considerations: Any shipwreck sunk for over three years in British Columbia waters is protected by law. Collection or salvage of any items is against the law.

Wreck of the Barnard Castle
Boat Dive

N

Bentinck Island

Pilot Bay

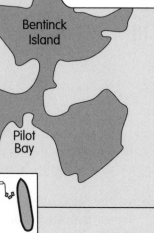

28 ft. deep

Small Moorage Buoy

⑤
⑥
Boilers
④

Barrels

⑦

③

The shaded areas represent the areas with the most concentrated wreckage.

⑧

The numbers shown on the diagram to the right correspond to plaques that have been placed around the wreck by the Underwater Archaeological Society of British Columbia (UASBC). The plaques denote the artifacts to be seen at that location.

②

Penetration of overhead environments such as caves, tunnels, or wrecks is dangerous. Do not enter unless you are properly trained.

①

40 ft. deep

Any wreck sunk for over three years in British Columbia waters is protected by law. Collection or salvage of any items is against the law.

This Map Is Not To Be Used For Navigation. Use only as a general guide for diving purposes.

Metchosin Area

SECTION III

Saanich Inlet

Many factors make the **Saanich Inlet** a unique marine environment. The characteristics of interest to divers are its lack of current, the extreme depth in a narrow inlet, its plankton blooms, and its relatively protected waters.

The Saanich Inlet has very weak currents. On large tidal exchanges you will feel only a slight pull of current, though the currents do get a little stronger as you move closer to the entrance of the inlet.

Although the currents are weak, the inlet contains a wide variety of marine life, from wolf eels, octopuses, six-gill sharks, and dog sharks to various other species of fish and invertebrates. You will also find some unusual invertebrates that like the weak currents of the Saanich Inlet—for example, cloud sponges.

The inlet's underwater topography is unique. Though most of the inlet is from 500 to 700 feet deep, at the mouth of the inlet the depths are only about 200 feet. It is this difference in depth that dictates only a small amount of water is exchanged with the tides. The resulting lack of water movement creates stagnant, lifeless, oxygen-depleted waters in the depths of the inlet. Because the inlet is so deep in such a narrow area, there are a lot of steep inclines and walls, as well as underwater valleys and mountains.

In the summer months, while other areas are experiencing bad visibility, the Saanich Inlet may have vis up to 30 metres (100 feet) or more. The summer sunshine can also make the inlet thick with plankton and algae, reducing the vis to near zero. These great variations in vis are also due to the lack of water movement and the extreme depth, as well as to nutrients that enter the inlet in the form of runoff from the surrounding land.

Another Saanich Inlet phenomenon is a "ceiling." The ceiling commonly occurs when plankton and algae form a layer in the upper water levels, usually at depths of 0 to 40 feet. In the ceiling you might be able to see only as far as a foot in front of you, while below the ceiling vis can be excellent. It is usually dark, however, so always dive with a flashlight.

The Saanich Inlet is sheltered on both sides by fairly high mountains. This means that when other places are windy, the inlet is quite often calm. It does not mean that it never gets rough. As you get closer to the entrance, the waters are much more exposed.

All of these special qualities make the Saanich Inlet one of my favourite places to dive when conditions at other sites are not good.

Shore Dives
Henderson Point
McKenzie Bight
Willis Point

Boat Dives
McCurdy Point
Senanus Island
Tozier Rock
White Lady (Repulse Rock)

Other Sites
Dyer Rocks
Patey Rock
Wain Rock

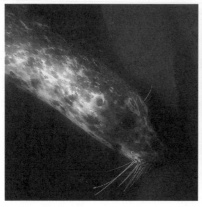

Friendly seal at McKenzie Bight

Boot sponge at Willis Point

Wolf eel at Tozier Rock

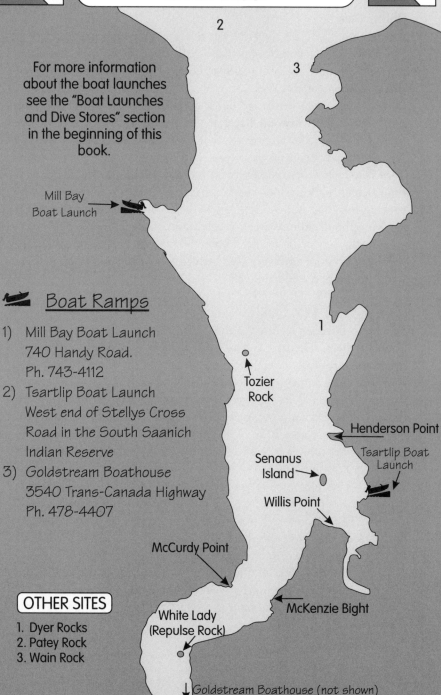

Saanich Inlet Overview

2

3

For more information about the boat launches see the "Boat Launches and Dive Stores" section in the beginning of this book.

Mill Bay Boat Launch

Boat Ramps

1) Mill Bay Boat Launch
   740 Handy Road.
   Ph. 743-4112

2) Tsartlip Boat Launch
   West end of Stellys Cross
   Road in the South Saanich
   Indian Reserve

3) Goldstream Boathouse
   3540 Trans-Canada Highway
   Ph. 478-4407

1

Tozier Rock

Henderson Point

Tsartlip Boat Launch

Senanus Island

Willis Point

McCurdy Point

McKenzie Bight

OTHER SITES

1. Dyer Rocks
2. Patey Rock
3. Wain Rock

White Lady
(Repulse Rock)

↓ Goldstream Boathouse (not shown)

Henderson Point

Shore Dive

Attractions: There are three reefs at this site, all with a good variety of life. I have seen many octopus dens at all three of the reefs and many times I've found the occupants at home. I have also heard tales of shark sightings at this site.

Directions: From Victoria, go north on West Saanich Road. Continue north through Brentwood Bay and the Tsartlip Indian Reserve. After passing through the reserve you will come to a road that is Mount Newton Cross Road on your right and Senanus Drive on your left. Turn left. Follow Senanus Drive all the way to its end, where you will find a small parking lot. The beach access is at the west end of the parking lot. The trail leading to the beach is about 60 metres (200 feet) long and culminates in a treacherous 1.5-metre (5 or 6 foot) drop to the beach. *Be careful.* Please park considerately; on a weekend there can be a lot of divers (and residents) at this site. Obey parking signs and respect residents.

    Latitude-48° 35.9'

    Longitude-123° 28.8'

Where To Dive: As mentioned above, there are three reefs worth having a look at here. The first reef is fairly shallow and smaller, while the other two are a little farther out and are almost like one big reef, though there is some space between them. I usually do a circuit around the two far reefs as if they were one. If you go straight out from the beach and a little to your right (255-degree compass heading), you will cross a sandy area 30 to 50 feet deep. After the sandy area you will come across a couple of reefs. Circumnavigating these reefs will take up about a 30-minute dive.

Current: The only current you are likely to encounter here is wind-driven current near the surface. It is not uncommon but is never strong.

Depths: The shallow reef is about 30 feet deep. The side of the two farther reefs that faces the shore is at about 45 feet. The back side of these reefs goes down to about 80 feet.

Hazards: The biggest hazard at this site is the drop at the end of the trail that leads onto the beach. There is also a boat launch around the corner in Brentwood Bay, and the boats really zip past Henderson Point, so use a dive flag!

Henderson Point
Shore Dive

Over 90 ft.

60-90 ft.

30-60 ft.

0-30 ft.

Parking Lot

House

Reef

255 degrees

Reef

Foot Path

Beach
(Entry & Exit Point)

House

Reef

There are three reefs worth having a look at. The first one is fairly shallow and smaller. The other two are a little farther out and are almost like one big reef, although there is some space in between them. I usually do a circuit around both. I have always had good luck spotting octopus at this site, so check out all the possible den sites closely.

This Map Is Not To Be Used For Navigation.
Use only as a general guide for diving purposes.

Saanich Inlet

McKenzie Bight

Boat Dive (Shore Dive?)

Attractions: One fine July day a friend and I were gearing up for a dive when we overheard a couple of guys talking exuberantly about a large shark they had just seen. We said, "Yeah right." One week later the same buddy and I were diving in the same spot and came across a very large six-gill shark. It was resting on the bottom in a sandy area at about 85 feet. Since our sighting I have heard of other shark sightings in the Saanich Inlet, especially near McKenzie Bight. I have also seen another six-gill at McKenzie Bight (not quite as big as the first one) and am now forced to believe every shark story that I hear.

On another dive we set out to find a known octopus den. We found the den, with the resident at home. We watched her for a while, then decided to move on. As we moved to the back of the den we saw another octopus, out in the open, with one tentacle disappearing under the rocks that made up the den. The octopus on the outside was in a trance-like state and was completely still except where its skin was rippling as it expelled water, which is their way of breathing. We assumed they were mating and I would guess we were right because a while later we went back and found the female octopus in her den, fanning a strings of eggs.

I have also had many dives at McKenzie Bight where the visibility was bad, there was not much life to see, or both.

Directions: McKenzie Bight is a little south of the actual dive sites. I say dive *sites* because there are at least three different places to dive from the shore at McKenzie Bight, indicated on the map as #1, #2, and #3.

I have designated this site as a "Boat Dive (Shore Dive?)" because recently a gate has been installed to close off the road access to the shore dive sites. Apparently too many rowdy people (*not* divers) were using the road at night as a party site. I am hoping that the dive shops will be able to negotiate with local residents and the municipality to get a key for the gate so that divers will once again have access to this site from shore. I have heard from some adventurous divers that they are parking at the gate and walking down to #1. People are permitted to walk in, but it is a bit of a hike.

By boat, launch at the Tsartlip Indian Reserve boat launch. Once you are launched, go south down Saanich Inlet. When you are out of Brentwood Bay, keep to the left and watch for McKenzie Bight on

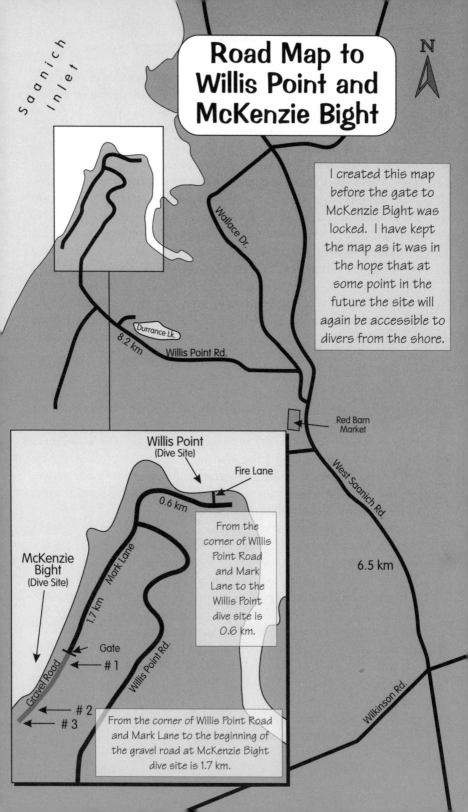

Road Map to Willis Point and McKenzie Bight

N

Saanich Inlet

I created this map before the gate to McKenzie Bight was locked. I have kept the map as it was in the hope that at some point in the future the site will again be accessible to divers from the shore.

Wallace Dr.

Durrance Lk.

8.2 km

Willis Point Rd.

Red Barn Market

Willis Point (Dive Site)

Fire Lane

0.6 km

From the corner of Willis Point Road and Mark Lane to the Willis Point dive site is 0.6 km.

West Saanich Rd.

6.5 km

McKenzie Bight (Dive Site)

Mark Lane

1.7 km

Gravel Road

Gate #1

Willis Point Rd.

#2

#3

From the corner of Willis Point Road and Mark Lane to the beginning of the gravel road at McKenzie Bight dive site is 1.7 km.

Wilkinson Rd.

your left. Remember that the dive sites are slightly north of the bight. Unfortunately there are no real landmarks to indicate which spot is which. All I can suggest is that if you stay out from shore about 100 metres, you will be able to see the rocks that block the end of the road.

By car, go north from Victoria on the Pat Bay Highway (#17). Turn left onto Royal Oak Drive at the Royal Oak overpass, turn right onto West Saanich Road, and go 6.5 kilometres north to Wallace Drive. Turn left onto Wallace Drive and go 0.5 kilometres to Willis Point Road. Once on Willis Point Road, go 8.2 kilometres to Mark Lane. Turn left on Mark Lane and drive 1.7 kilometres to the gate where the gravel road starts. If the gravel road at the end of Mark Lane is opened up again, you will find it is unserviced and very rough, with parts of it washed away. There are also a lot of overhanging trees. It is best to tackle this with a truck, but I have seen cars there. **Special Note:** When you are at about the 4-kilometre mark on Willis Point Road you will come across a sign saying "McKenzie Bight (turn left)." **Don't turn**; this is only a hiking trail to McKenzie Bight.

Latitude-48° 33.5'

Longitude-123° 30.3'

Where To Dive: I have entered the water at spots along the whole stretch of the gravel road and found all sites to be similar. The main concern is easy access to the water from the road. There are three popular spots (see the map). The first spot is approximately 200 metres past the end of the pavement; the second is approximately 600 metres past the end of the pavement; and the third is at the end of the lane, where boulders block the road.

Current: None to speak of.

Depths: The bottom contour at the #1 spot is deceiving as there is a trench that goes down to about 90 feet. You can be swimming at a depth of 50 feet, heading out or coming back to shore, when all of a sudden the bottom starts getting deeper, so be prepared to swim in mid-water without being able to see the bottom or the surface. The other two spots deepen gradually in the shallow areas and have walls and steep drop-offs in the deeper areas. Maximum depth is whatever you wish, but most of the good stuff is 80 feet or shallower.

Hazards: Deep drop-offs, bad vis, jellyfish in the fall, and man-eating sharks (just kidding).

Other Considerations: Divers should be very considerate of locals at this site in an attempt to regain road access.

McKenzie Bight
Boat Dive (Shore Dive?)

N

If you are lucky you may see a six-gill shark. They come from the depths in the summer months, supposedly to feed in the shallower water ("shallower" being 80 feet or deeper).

A stream crosses the road here and has partly washed out the road.

Parking Area

Over 120 ft.

90-120 ft.

60-90 ft.

30-60 ft.

0-30 ft.

#1

#2

#3

#4

Large Boulders

As I was writing this book, a gate was installed near the beginning of the gravel road. I hope that some arrangement can be made to give divers access to this site again.

Saanich Inlet

This Map Is Not To Be Used For Navigation.
Use only as a general guide for diving purposes.

Willis Point

Shore Dive

Attractions: A sheer wall starts at a depth of approximately 35 feet and drops to about 130 feet. In the deeper depths there are large boot sponges, many of which are tagged for research by University of Victoria scientists. There are also some cloud sponges at the western end of the wall. Unfortunately they are not in very good shape. From shore to the top of the wall, hidden in the leaf kelp, there are many smaller creatures to be discovered. Safety stops are rarely boring.

Directions: From Victoria, go north on the Pat Bay Highway (#17). Turn left onto Royal Oak Drive at the Royal Oak overpass, turn right onto West Saanich Road, and go 6.5 kilometres north to Wallace Drive. Turn left onto Wallace Drive and go 0.5 kilometres to Willis Point Road. Once on Willis Point Road, go 8.2 kilometres to Mark Lane. Turn right on Mark Lane and drive 0.6 kilometres to a fire service lane on your left. Do not park in the fire lane or block it in any way; you can park on Mark Lane near the entrance to the fire lane. The address of the last house on your left before the fire lane is 7442 Mark Lane. Please have consideration for residents, as parking is limited.

Latitude-48° 34.7'

Longitude-123° 29.1'

Where To Dive: From the end of the fire lane, go out about 18 metres (60 feet), submerge, go straight out (north) until the bottom drops off steeply, and then turn left (west). If you go to the right, the wall turns into sloping bottom. I usually go out to the wall, go down to my maximum depth, follow the wall for a while, then turn around and follow the wall back at a shallower depth. With this method I never see anything twice.

Current: Not much at all.

Depths: The top of the wall starts at approximately 35 feet. The deepest part of the wall is about 130 feet.

Hazards: Steep drop-off, bad vis, boats (a large marina and a boat launch are nearby), and jellyfish.

Other Considerations: Please be very careful around all marine life, especially the boot and cloud sponges.

Willis Point
Shore Dive

There are numerous boot sponges starting at about 80 feet deep. UVic students and scientists are studying these sponges and have tagged them for the purposes of their studies. They already know that the growth rate of all sponges is very slow and are trying to determine the exact growth rate and ages of the boot sponges.

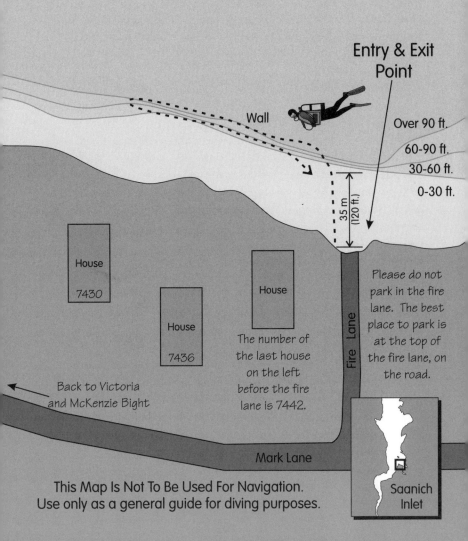

Entry & Exit Point

Wall

Over 90 ft.

60-90 ft.

30-60 ft.

0-30 ft.

35 m (120 ft.)

House 7430

House

House 7436

The number of the last house on the left before the fire lane is 7442.

Fire Lane

Please do not park in the fire lane. The best place to park is at the top of the fire lane, on the road.

Back to Victoria and McKenzie Bight

Mark Lane

Saanich Inlet

This Map Is Not To Be Used For Navigation.
Use only as a general guide for diving purposes.

McCurdy Point

Boat Dive

Attractions: Octopuses are abundant at McCurdy Point and are usually in dens. Cloud sponges as big as Volkswagen Beetles inhabit the depths. The underwater topography is amazing. When I dove this site one summer day in early September, the visibility from the surface to 40 feet deep was about 9 metres (30 feet). Below 40 feet I could see 30 metres (100 feet). We could see towering mountain ranges, deep valleys, and schools of dogfish off in the distance. What a day! Unfortunately, not all my dives at McCurdy Point have been that good.

Directions: Launch at the Tsartlip Indian Reserve boat launch. Once you are launched, go south down the Saanich Inlet. McCurdy Point is on your right.

Latitude-48° 33.7'

Longitude-123° 31.2'

Where To Dive: I usually anchor right at McCurdy Point and go west or north. You can find cloud sponges just west of the point, as indicated on the map. A sloping wall goes down to about 40 feet, where there is a plateau with sand and shell bottom. This is a good place to find octopus dens. At the edge of the plateau is a series of valleys that run at approximately 45-degree angles to the shore. In between the valleys, a wall (sometimes sloping, sometimes vertical) falls into the inky black abyss.

Current: None.

Depths: The sandy plateau is at about 40 feet. The valley bottoms vary in depth, but the average is about 90 feet. And the bottom of the wall is...

Hazards: Because it gets steep in such a short distance, there is very little room to anchor. If you keep your anchor line too short, you may drag anchor and your boat will be gone when you come up. If you put out too much line, your boat may end up bouncing off the rocks. To make matters worse, if there is any wind in the inlet, McCurdy Point gets the brunt of it. This means it is even more important for you to have good anchorage. I use an inflatable boat so I don't mind if it bounces off the rocks, but if you have any other kind of craft you may want to take someone along to sit in the boat.

Other Considerations: It is usually a good idea to get a visibility report from a local dive shop. If vis is really bad, it is not worth going.

McCurdy Point
Boat Dive

N

McCurdy Point is a great spot if you like spectacular underwater topography. If you dive here when the visibility is above average (over 50 feet), you will be treated to walls and valleys the likes of which I have not seen anywhere else.

McCurdy Point

0-30 ft.

30-60 ft.

60-90 ft.

Over 90 ft.

Anchor right at McCurdy Point and then go west or north from there.

You can find cloud sponges in the area around where the diver is shown above. Please be careful when you are looking at cloud sponges as they are delicate and grow very slowly. Slight contact can damage them.

This Map Is Not To Be Used For Navigation.
Use only as a general guide for diving purposes.

Saanich Inlet

Senanus Island

Boat Dive

Attractions: Senanus Island has the most concentrated population of cloud sponges that I have seen anywhere. Cloud sponges have always intrigued me because of their unusual growth formations, and this site is an excellent place to see the variety of unique shapes. Many of the sponges are dead or dying, but there are also a lot of them in good shape. (My friend the marine biologist says that the sponges may be dying as part of their natural life cycle, but we don't know enough about them to be sure. One thing is certain, though, and that is that any physical contact by divers is fatal to the portion of the sponge that is touched, so be careful!)

Directions: Launch at the Tsartlip Indian Reserve boat launch. Senanus Island is straight out from the boat launch.

Latitude-48° 35.6'

Longitude-123° 29.0'

Where To Dive: Off the northwest corner of the island there is a reef that goes down very deep. This reef is where you will find the cloud sponges, along with various other life. A depth sounder will help you locate the reef. (See the map for details.)

Current: As in the rest of the Saanich Inlet, the current is weak or non-existent.

Depths: Depending on where you anchor, the top of the reef is at about 30 feet. The cloud sponges start at 90 feet and go down to at least 130 feet.

Hazards: On a windy day, or on a day with a large tidal exchange, there can be enough current to take you a long way from the boat during your safety stop, which will be in mid-water. I always ensure that I know how to make my way back to the anchor line so that I can do my safety stop while in sight of the rope. It is a good idea to tie some sort of reflective, highly visible flag on the anchor line about 1 or 2 metres (5 or 6 feet) from the bottom to make it easier to find on your return.

Senanus Island
Boat Dive

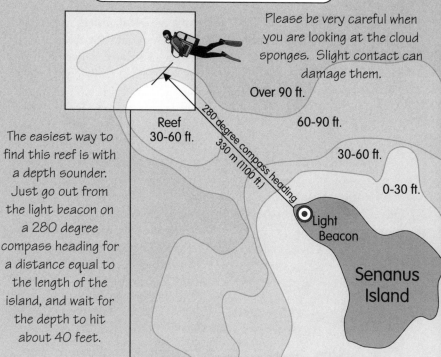

Please be very careful when you are looking at the cloud sponges. Slight contact can damage them.

Over 90 ft.

60-90 ft.

Reef
30-60 ft.

30-60 ft.

0-30 ft.

The easiest way to find this reef is with a depth sounder. Just go out from the light beacon on a 280 degree compass heading for a distance equal to the length of the island, and wait for the depth to hit about 40 feet.

280 degree compass heading
330 m (1100 ft.)

Light Beacon

Senanus Island

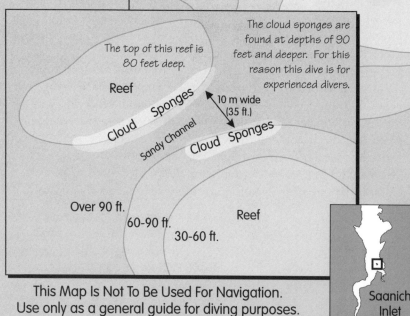

The top of this reef is 80 feet deep.

Reef

Cloud Sponges

Sandy Channel

10 m wide (35 ft.)

Cloud Sponges

The cloud sponges are found at depths of 90 feet and deeper. For this reason this dive is for experienced divers.

Over 90 ft.

60-90 ft.

30-60 ft.

Reef

Saanich Inlet

This Map Is Not To Be Used For Navigation.
Use only as a general guide for diving purposes.

Tozier Rock

Boat Dive

Attractions: Scarface is one of a group of wolf eels that lives near Tozier Rock. At one time there were as many as seven, and the fewest that I have seen there is two. Last time I dived here I counted five of them. These wolf eels, especially Scarface, are accustomed to divers. On one dive we were having trouble finding their den until one wolf eel found us and led us to their home. Divers have made a habit of feeding these wolf eels, and because of this they have become quite bold. I don't condone feeding them because it creates unnatural behaviour that can be unnerving for someone not prepared for the experience. Please respect these amazing creatures and remember they are *wild* animals despite their Muppet-like appearance.

Directions: Launch at the Tsartlip Indian Reserve boat launch. Once launched, go north through Saanich Inlet and just past the Mill Bay Ferry landing. On your left is Tozier Rock. There is a marker on the rock, and at low tide there is some rock showing, but not a lot. Anchor south-southeast of the marker, about 60 metres (200 feet) out. Your anchor should be in about 9 to 12 metres (30 to 40 feet) of water.

Latitude-48° 37.1'

Longitude-123° 30.8'

Where To Dive: There is a wall that runs parallel to shore on the east side of the marker. It starts at around 70 feet and seems to go down forever. I don't usually check out this wall because when I dive at Tozier Rock, all my time is spent with the wolf eels.

To find the wolf eels: anchor about 60 metres (200 feet) south of the marker. Go down and follow the reef going south, keeping your depth at around 65 feet. On your right you will see a small valley filled with boulders. You will find the wolf eels where the valley spills down into the face of a small wall.

Current: There is occasional light tidal current.

Depths: The wolf eels are at 65 to 75 feet.

Hazards: Beware of the wind; it can really whip up on this side of the inlet.

Tozier Rock
Boat Dive

N

0-30 ft.	30-60 ft.	60-80 ft.	80-100 ft.	100-130 ft.	Over 130 ft.

Tozier Rock Marker

Rocky Area

Sandy Area

Ledge

80 ft.

Wolf Eels

Sandy Area

65 ft.

50 ft.

Rock

Rocky Area

135 degree compass heading
84 m (275 ft.)

Reef

Wolf eel dens at 70 feet deep

Good spot to anchor

Any time I have gone to Tozier Rock I have seen at least two wolf eels, but at one time there were as many as seven wolf eels found here consistently.

This Map Is Not To Be Used For Navigation.
Use only as a general guide for diving purposes.

Saanich Inlet

White Lady (Repulse Rock)

Boat Dive

Attractions: There is a good variety of underwater terrain, lots of larger fish, and crabs galore at this site. To the southwest, in the deeper areas, are a number of cloud sponges at least 1 metre (3 feet) in diameter. Big jellyfish with 9-metre-long (30 feet) tails are also common.

Directions: Launch at the Tsartlip Indian Reserve boat launch or the Goldstream Boathouse. From the Indian Reserve go south down the inlet to Repulse Rock. From the Goldstream Boathouse go north to Repulse Rock. There is a marker on Repulse Rock and, depending on the tide height, a fair piece of rock showing.

Latitude-48° 32.8'

Longitude-123° 32.3'

Where To Dive: To the southwest are steeper drop-offs. The cloud sponges that I have seen are to the south of the marker, at depths below 100 feet. I usually anchor near the marker and then go south to the cloud sponges.

Current: None.

Depths: The cloud sponges are at around 120 feet deep on the wall, to the south of the marker.

Hazards: I have seen fishing boats almost circling this rock, so don't get hooked! I have never seen so many jellyfish on a single dive as there were on one dive in late summer at the White Lady.

Cloud sponge

White Lady
(Repulse Rock)
Boat Dive

Cloud sponges can be found in the area around the diver. Please be careful when you are looking at the cloud sponges as they are very delicate and grow slowly. Slight contact can damage them.

For the beginning diver, there is a lot to see in the shallower areas around the marker.

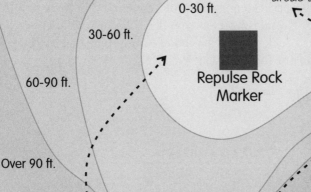

0-30 ft.

30-60 ft.

60-90 ft.

Over 90 ft.

Repulse Rock Marker

Wall

Wall

The dashed line indicates a route that would be good for the more advanced diver. The deeper walls and valleys found to the south of the marker are where the cloud sponges can be seen.

This Map Is Not To Be Used For Navigation. Use only as a general guide for diving purposes.

Saanich Inlet

Other Sites

Boat Dives

Here are a few other dives to check out in the Saanich Inlet.

Dyer Rocks
Latitude-48° 37.4'
Longitude-123° 29.0'

Patey Rock
Latitude-48° 42.0'
Longitude-123° 31.2'

I have heard of people swimming out from shore to **Wain Rock**, but it is a tough swim. I would not even consider going from shore, but if you want to have a look, park at the end of Moses Point Road and take the trail that leads to the beach.
Latitude-48° 41.3'
Longitude-123° 29.3'

SECTION IV

Sidney Area

The big attraction in the **Sidney** area of late is the HMCS *MacKenzie*. Divers flock to the ship by the thousands every year. It is a great first or second dive depending on the currents. However, there are many other sites in the area that are overlooked because everyone wants to dive on the *MacKenzie*. Little-known sites like Graham's Wall (lots of life and little current) or Rubly Island are great places to dive. In my opinion, the best dive in the area is North Cod Reef, which is on a par with Race Rocks (see "Metchosin Area") except that there are no sea lions and it is, arguably, not quite as diverse in the invertebrate department. Of the dives listed in "Other Sites," I particularly like Arachne Reef and Joan Rock.

I enjoy diving in this area during the summer. You can relax between dives at Sidney Spit or one of the other two marine parks in the area—Isle-de-Lis (which can be seen on the map of HMCS *MacKenzie*) and Princess Margaret Marine Park (on the map of the *G.B. Church*).

Shore Dives
Sidney Pier

Boat Dives
Arbutus Island
G.B. Church (Artificial Reef)
Graham's Wall
HMCS *MacKenzie* (Artificial Reef)
North Cod Reef
Rubly Island

Other Sites
Arachne Reef
Canoe Rock

Other Sites (continued)

Cooper Reef
Forest Island
Imrie Island
Joan Rock
Little Group Islands
Reay Island
Sidney Spit
South Cod Reef

Sidney Area Overview

For more information about the boat launches see the "Boat Launches and Dive Stores" section in the beginning of this book.

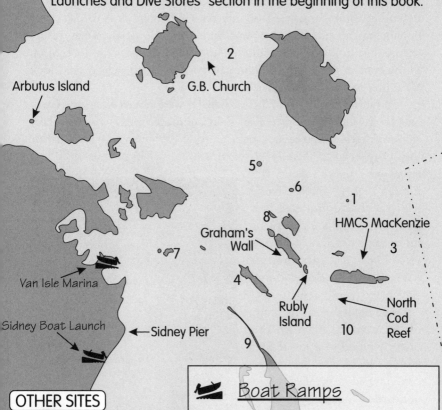

Arbutus Island

G.B. Church

2

5

6

1

HMCS MacKenzie

3

8

Graham's Wall

7

Van Isle Marina

4

Rubly Island

North Cod Reef

Sidney Boat Launch

Sidney Pier

9

10

OTHER SITES

1. Arachne Reef
2. Canoe Rock
3. Cooper Reef
4. Forest Island
5. Imrie Island
6. Joan Rock
7. Little Group Islands
8. Reay Island
9. Sidney Spit
10. South Cod Reef

Boat Ramps

1) Van Isle Marina
   2320 Harbour Road
   Ph. 656-1138
2) Sidney Boat Launch
   9500 block of Lochside Drive
   (right beside the Anacortes Ferry)
3) Island View Beach Boat Launch
   End of Island View Road

Island View Beach Boat Launch

Sidney Pier

Shore Dive

Attractions: In 1996 the Town of Sidney built a 96-metre (320 foot) pier at the end of Bevan Avenue for such recreational uses as fishing, scuba diving, nature viewing, and scenic walks. The town has plans to extend the pier another 100 metres (330 feet) and to continue enhancing the site. The pier was built using donated money rather than public funds. If you would like to make a donation to the project, please contact the Town of Sidney or go to http://dive.bc.ca and look for a link to the "Sidney Pier."

In November 1996, 270 Reef Balls™ were placed along the north and south sides of the pier. Reef Balls are made from environmentally stable concrete mixtures and make an ideal habitat for fish and marine life. They weigh 170 to 340 kilograms (375 to 750 pounds) each and are about 1 metre wide by 0.5 metres high (3 by 1.5 feet). Along with the proposed pier extension, there are also plans for another artificial Reef Ball reef. For more information have a look at the Reef Ball web site, http://www.reefball.org/.

The natural reef just south of the wharf (shown on the map) is home to a lot of life, which seems to be more concentrated at the deeper end of the reef. The life on the Reef Balls is still pretty sparse but is increasing rapidly. In the summer, leaf kelp can cover the balls, making it hard to see anything.

Directions: From Victoria, go north on Pat Bay Highway (#17) until you come to the traffic lights at the town of Sidney (Beacon Avenue). Turn right and follow Beacon

Sea pen

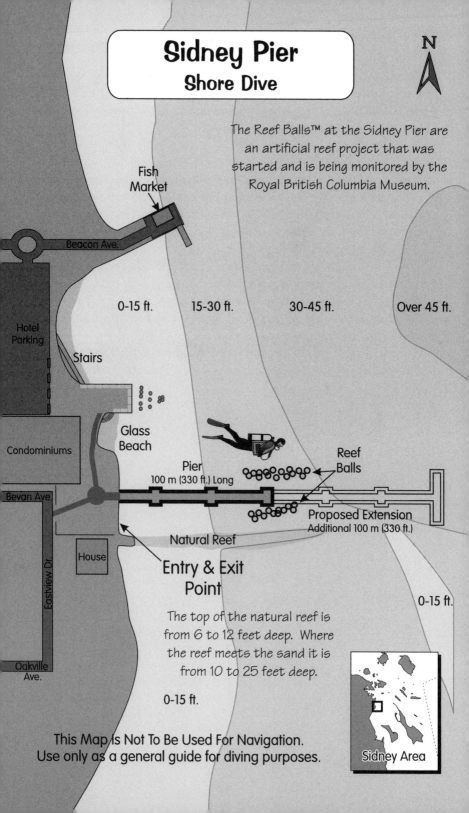

Sidney Pier
Shore Dive

N

The Reef Balls™ at the Sidney Pier are an artificial reef project that was started and is being monitored by the Royal British Columbia Museum.

Fish Market

Beacon Ave.

0-15 ft.   15-30 ft.   30-45 ft.   Over 45 ft.

Hotel Parking

Stairs

Glass Beach

Condominiums

Pier
100 m (330 ft.) Long

Reef Balls

Proposed Extension
Additional 100 m (330 ft.)

Bevan Ave.

Eastview Dr.

House

Natural Reef

Entry & Exit Point

0-15 ft.

The top of the natural reef is from 6 to 12 feet deep. Where the reef meets the sand it is from 10 to 25 feet deep.

Oakville Ave.

0-15 ft.

This Map Is Not To Be Used For Navigation.
Use only as a general guide for diving purposes.

Sidney Area

Avenue almost to the end, turning right on First Street. Then take your first left, which is Bevan Avenue. Bevan runs for one block and ends. At the end of Bevan, turn right onto Eastview Drive and park. If you look towards the ocean you will see the wharf.

Latitude-48° 38.8'

Longitude-123° 23.5'

Where to Dive: Enter the water on either side of the wharf, but be careful getting down the rocks. You can easily take in the natural reef and do a tour of the Reef Balls with plenty of time left over.

Current: Two-knot currents occur at this site, so dive at slack on large tidal exchanges. On smaller tidal exchanges you will have a lot more leeway with the currents, but always check the tide tables and assess conditions before entering the water.

Depths: You will either have to swim out a long way or dig a hole to get much deeper than 30 feet. The top of the reef is from 6 to 12 feet deep while the reef meets the sand at 10 to 25 feet.

Hazards: People fishing on the wharf could hook you, and although the wharf is not for mooring, there is a lot of boat traffic in the area.

Arbutus Island

Boat Dive

Attractions: This is an easy dive with a wide variety of underwater terrain and life. There is a shallow cave (more like an overhang) that has attracted a lot of life.

Directions: Use the Sidney boat launch to get to Arbutus Island. Be sure to check your chart when travelling through this area, as there are a lot of shallow spots. Go north to the northern tip of the Saanich Peninsula and then turn west. Continue on a westward course past the BC Ferries dock and past Piers Island. On the east side of Piers Island you will see a small island with a few scraggly trees. You have found Arbutus Island.

  Latitude-48° 42.4'

  Longitude-123° 26.1'

Where To Dive: The best part of the dive is at the west-southwest end of the island, but it is worth going around and seeing the east and north sides of the island. The south side is very shallow and there is not much to see. The small cave is at the southwest corner of the island in about 15 feet of water.

Hermit crab

Current: The current in Satellite Channel is not very strong but it can make diving difficult. It is best to dive at slack tide, but I have gone later and earlier and been able to dive with no problem. Definitely dive at slack on a large tidal exchange. If you are not diving at slack it is a good idea to have a live boat.

Hazards: A BC Ferries route goes right around Arbutus Island. The ferry does not get close enough to cause concern, but it can create big waves that will make your boat drag anchor. (I know this from experience!)

Cabezon sculpin

Arbutus Island
Boat Dive

There is a small cave (tunnel) in
about 15 feet of water on the
island's southwest corner.

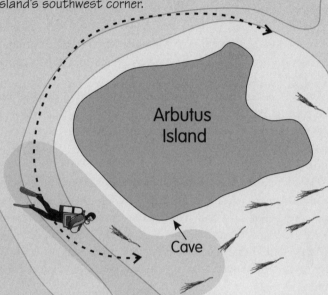

Arbutus
Island

Cave

The shaded area on the map
marks the area where the life
and the underwater terrain
are the most interesting.

Over 100 ft.   60-100 ft.   30-60 ft.   0-30 ft.

Penetration of overhead environments
such as caves, tunnels, or wrecks is
dangerous. Do not enter unless you
are properly trained.

This Map Is Not To Be Used For Navigation.
Use only as a general guide for diving purposes.

Sidney Area

G.B. Church (Artificial Reef)

Boat Dive

Attractions: The *G.B. Church* is a 50-metre (165 foot) freighter that was sunk in 1991 by the Artificial Reef Society of British Columbia. Since then the wreck has become a beacon for life. Although there is not much current here, which usually signals lack of life, the wreck provides a place for animals to hide and live. The *G.B. Church* was sunk just off Portland Island in Princess Margaret Marine Park. Portland is a beautiful island and an ideal place to have lunch or even to camp overnight.

Directions: Launch at the Sidney boat launch. The *G.B. Church* is on the southeast side of Portland Island. The buoys for the *G.B. Church* are shown on the newer Canadian Hydrographic Service charts.

Latitude-48° 40.2'

Longitude-123° 17.2'

Where To Dive: There are several marker buoys and several anchorage buoys. The anchorage buoys are around the outside of the ship. The marker buoys are labelled bow and stern and are attached to the top of the mast on the bow and the top of the mast on the stern respectively. Go down at either of these markers and come up at the other. It is relatively easy to find your way back up the marker buoy chains, even in bad visibility.

For beginning divers I would recommend going down and coming up on the stern marker buoy. The stern portion of the ship has more to see above the 60-foot mark.

Current: On larger tidal exchanges you must dive on slack, but on smaller tidal exchanges you will have a little more leeway with the current. It is easy to stay on the ship in a slight current, and you can ascend the chains to the marker buoys.

Depths: The bottom of the ship rests in an average of 90 feet of water on sandy bottom.

Hazards: Do not enter the wreck unless you are properly trained and equipped.

Other Considerations: Any shipwreck sunk for over three years in British Columbia waters is protected by law. Collection or salvage of any items is against the law.

G.B. Church
Boat Dive

N

Any wreck sunk for over three years in British Columbia waters is protected by law. Collection or salvage of any items is against the law.

Portland Island
(Princess Margaret Marine Park)

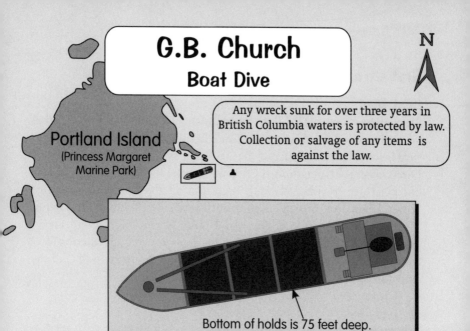

Bottom of holds is 75 feet deep.

There are 2 marker buoys at this site marking the bow (front) and the stern (rear). There are also several anchorage buoys. Please be cautious when approaching this site as divers often surface away from the wreck.

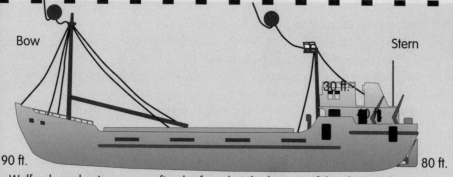

Bow

Stern

30 ft.

90 ft.

80 ft.

Wolf eels and octopus can often be found at the bottom of the ship on the sand.

Penetration of overhead environments such as caves, tunnels, or wrecks is dangerous. Do not enter unless you are properly trained.

This Map Is Not To Be Used For Navigation. Use only as a general guide for diving purposes.

Sidney Area

Graham's Wall

Boat Dive

Attractions: Graham's Wall is covered with anemones and various other life and is accessible most of the time. It is one of these rare spots with very little current and lots of life. A "must see."

Directions: Start out from the Sidney boat launch and go around the northern tip of Sidney Island, then around the southeastern tip of Forest Island. Go north to the southwest side of Domville Island. Midway down the side of the island there is a drying rock (dries on tides of 2.7 metres—9 feet—or lower) approximately 30 metres (100 feet) out from shore. This rock marks the location of the wall. See the map for exact details.

Latitude-48° 40.2'

Longitude-123° 19.3'

Where To Dive: The northwest end of the rock is the deeper area, so it is the best place to start. Work your way along the wall to the southeast, then finish the dive by continuing on around north of the rock and back to the boat.

Current: Always check conditions on arrival at the site. The following are general guidelines for diving at Graham's Wall, but there may be conditions when these guidelines do not apply.

- On a small tidal exchange you can dive anytime.
- On a medium tidal exchange you can dive anytime except maximum flood or ebb. (Maximum flood or ebb is the time when the current has reached its peak speed.)
- On a large tidal exchange you can dive at slack and maybe a little on either side of slack.

Depths: The deepest part of the wall is about 100 feet deep.

Graham's Wall
Boat Dive

Domville Island

Graham's Wall

Domville Island

The drying rock dries on tides lower than 2.7 metres (9 feet). This means that some part of this rock is visible most times except during very high tides, and even then you can usually spot the waves lapping around the top of the rock.

Possible Entry & Exit Point

Good spot to anchor

Drying Rock

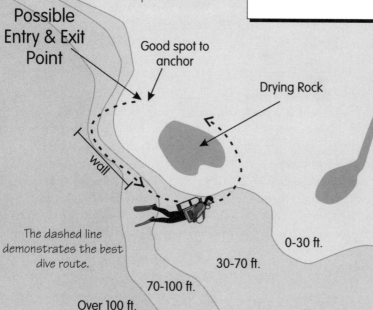

wall

The dashed line demonstrates the best dive route.

0-30 ft.

30-70 ft.

70-100 ft.

Over 100 ft.

This Map Is Not To Be Used For Navigation.
Use only as a general guide for diving purposes.

Sidney Area

HMCS *MacKenzie* (Artificial Reef)

Boat Dive

Attractions: The 110-metre (366 foot) destroyer from the Canadian Navy was sunk on September 16, 1995, by the Artificial Reef Society of British Columbia. The society stripped the ship of any toxic materials and then made it as safe as possible for divers, cutting holes all over the wreck so divers can enter. Exploring this enormous wreck is an exhilarating experience. Even if you are not trained in wreck diving, you can still make a few dives to explore the exterior of the ship (most of the marine life is around the exterior). And if you *are* trained in wreck diving, you can spend weeks exploring the labyrinthine interior of the ship.

Marine life has already begun to invade the wreck, even though it has only been underwater for a relatively short time. In the years to come the amount of life will just keep getting better and better.

The *MacKenzie* is north of Gooch Island. At the east end of Gooch is Rum Island, which is actually attached to Gooch by a small strip of land. Rum Island is part of Isle-de-Lis Marine Park. A scenic trail goes all the way around Rum Island, and the beach that connects Rum to Gooch is a great lunch spot.

Directions: Use the Sidney boat launch and go around the northern tip of Sidney Island, then around the southeastern tip of Forest Island. Go northeast up to Gooch Island and then east through the channel between Comet and Gooch Islands. You can't miss the marker buoys from there.

Latitude-48° 40.2'
Longitude-123° 17.2'

Where To Dive: Please keep in mind that the following information is subject to change, as winter storms often break ropes, and buoys can be lost or moved. When this book went to press there were three marker buoys and three moorage buoys.

Moorage Buoys   Marker Buoys

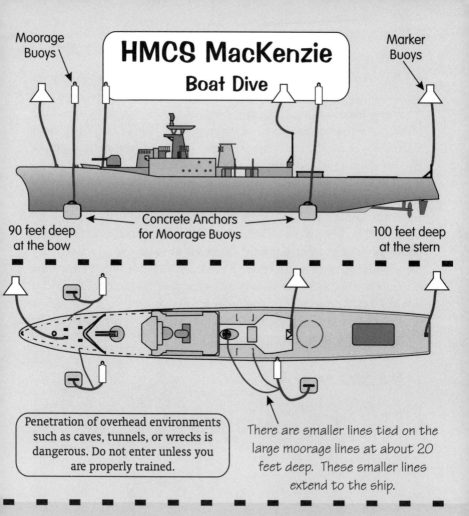

HMCS MacKenzie
Boat Dive

Moorage Buoys

Marker Buoys

Concrete Anchors for Moorage Buoys

90 feet deep at the bow

100 feet deep at the stern

Penetration of overhead environments such as caves, tunnels, or wrecks is dangerous. Do not enter unless you are properly trained.

There are smaller lines tied on the large moorage lines at about 20 feet deep. These smaller lines extend to the ship.

This ship was sunk in September 1995 to create an artificial reef for marine life and scuba divers alike.

N

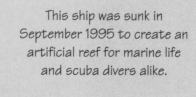

Rum Island (Isle-De-Lis Marine Park)

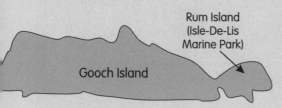

Gooch Island

This Map Is Not To Be Used For Navigation. Use only as a general guide for diving purposes.

Sidney Area

The moorage lines are anchored to large concrete blocks that sit on the bottom at approximately 100 feet deep. The best way to get to the ship is to descend along a moorage buoy line until you get to one of the smaller lines that are tied onto the moorage buoy lines at a depth of about 30 feet. These smaller lines extend roughly horizontally from the moorage lines to the ship to facilitate easy access to the wreck. When you get to the ship be sure to make a mental note of where the horizontal line is attached. If you take the wrong line back to the surface and there is a current, it could be difficult getting back to your boat.

Current: The best time to dive is at slack or on a flood tide. During a flood tide the current is partly deflected around the *MacKenzie* by Gooch Island, though this is not a hard and fast rule. On a large tidal exchange there can be strong currents even on a flood tide. On an ebb tide the *MacKenzie* is hit straight on by the current, so unless it is a small exchange it is not possible to dive. As with all dive sites, arrive early and assess the currents before entering the water.

Peering into the HMCS MacKenzie

Depths: The bottom of the ship rests in an average of 90 to 100 feet of water and is listing approximately 15 degrees to port. Because of the list to port, the port side is about 10 feet deeper than the starboard side.

At midship, on the port side—
- the radar tower is 35 feet deep,
- Deck A is 45 feet deep,
- Deck 1 is 60 feet deep,
- Deck 2 is 70 feet deep,
- Deck 3 is 80 feet deep,
- Deck 4 is 90 feet deep, and
- Deck 5 is 100 feet deep.

I suggest that you stick to Deck 3 or shallower. The bottom two decks are more dangerous than any of the other decks for a few reasons.

Silt: When silt gets stirred up on the decks above, it settles down into these decks. There are far fewer divers on these decks, so the silt that is here does not get stirred up and taken away by the current as it does on the decks above. When it is stirred up by a diver, the resulting "silt-out" can cause visibility to drop to near zero. If you are caught in a "silt-out," stay calm and remain still to allow the silt to settle.

Limited Access Holes: There are fewer access holes and there are some areas that are very tight. There are also places where you might think that you can get through because you can see light, but which are actually dead ends.

Increased Depth: The increased depth of the lower decks means you have much less bottom time in case of a problem.

Hazards: Do not enter the wreck unless you are properly trained and equipped. What looks easy can turn into tragedy very quickly.

Other Considerations: Any shipwreck sunk for over three years in British Columbia waters is protected by law. Collection or salvage of any items is against the law.

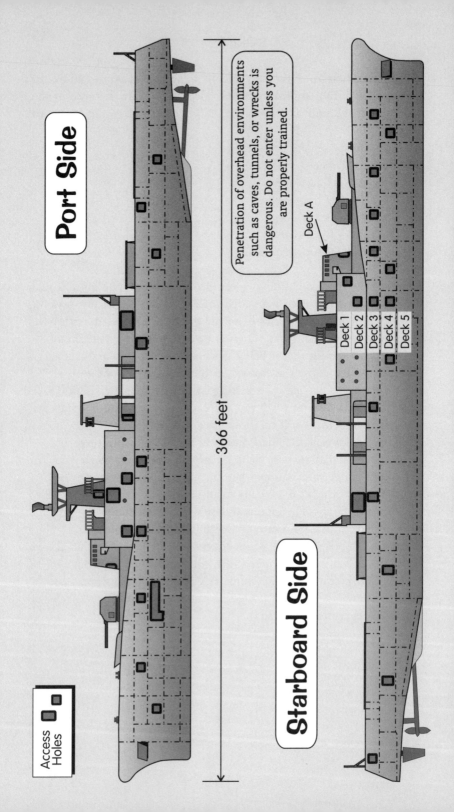

Port Side

Access
Holes

366 feet

Penetration of overhead environments such as caves, tunnels, or wrecks is dangerous. Do not enter unless you are properly trained.

Deck A

Deck 1
Deck 2
Deck 3
Deck 4
Deck 5

Starboard Side

Note: These two decks do not run the full length of the ship.

Horizontal Access Holes ⊥ ⊢

Vertical Access Holes ■ ● ■

Walls That Have Been Removed ┈┈┈

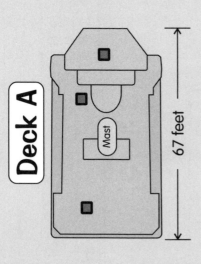

Deck A

Mast

67 feet

Penetration of overhead environments such as caves, tunnels, or wrecks is dangerous. Do not enter unless you are properly trained.

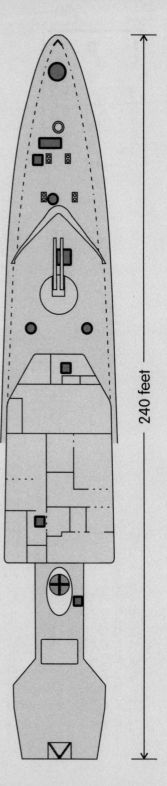

Deck 1

240 feet

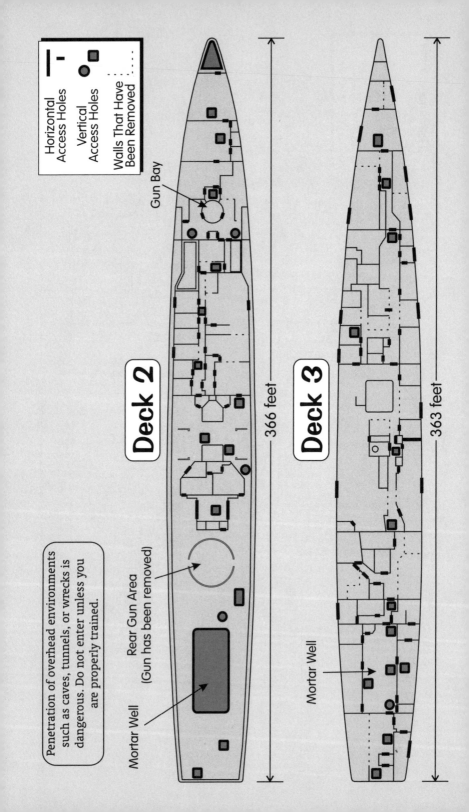

Horizontal Access Holes ▬

Vertical Access Holes ● ■

Walls That Have Been Removed ⋯⋯

Gun Bay

Deck 2

366 feet

Penetration of overhead environments such as caves, tunnels, or wrecks is dangerous. Do not enter unless you are properly trained.

Mortar Well

Rear Gun Area (Gun has been removed)

Deck 3

363 feet

Mortar Well

Penetration of overhead environments such as caves, tunnels, or wrecks is dangerous. Do not enter unless you are properly trained.

Deck 4

358 feet

Deck 5

354 feet

These decks are more dangerous than any of the other decks, which is why I have not shown the access holes. I suggest that you stick to Deck 3 or shallower.

North Cod Reef

Boat Dive

Attractions: There are actually two small reefs at this site, but if you are diving deeper than the channel between them (45 feet deep), they will seem like one big reef. Commonly seen "Big Stuff" is seals, king crabs, dogfish, cabezon, ling cod, and black cod. "Small Stuff" is just about everything found everywhere else put together. This is a great dive that never becomes boring no matter how many times you dive it. The only drawback is that I can never decide between a macro or wide angle lens for my camera.

Directions: Launch at the Sidney boat launch. North Cod Reef is south of the western tip of Gooch Island. At low tides below 0.6 metres (2 feet) the rock on the main reef dries (is visible).

Latitude-48° 39.5'

Longitude-123° 18.1'

Crimson anemone

North Cod Reef
Boat Dive

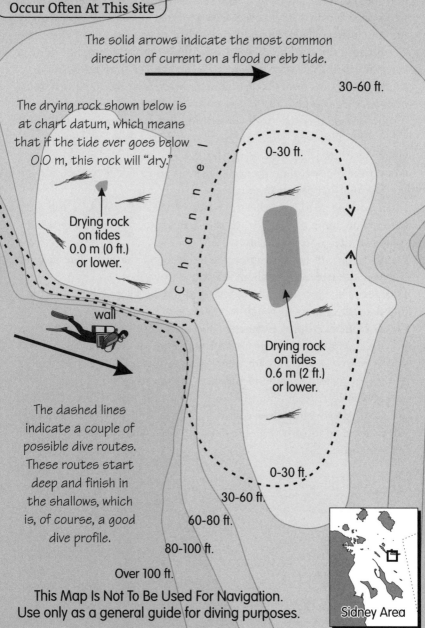

60-80 ft.

The solid arrows indicate the most common
direction of current on a flood or ebb tide.

30-60 ft.

The drying rock shown below is
at chart datum, which means
that if the tide ever goes below
0.0 m, this rock will "dry."

0-30 ft.

Channel

Drying rock
on tides
0.0 m (0 ft.)
or lower.

wall

Drying rock
on tides
0.6 m (2 ft.)
or lower.

The dashed lines
indicate a couple of
possible dive routes.
These routes start
deep and finish in
the shallows, which
is, of course, a good
dive profile.

0-30 ft.

30-60 ft.

60-80 ft.

80-100 ft.

Over 100 ft.

This Map Is Not To Be Used For Navigation.
Use only as a general guide for diving purposes.

Sidney Area

Where To Dive & Current: The current at this site is strong no matter how small the tidal exchange is, so arrive early and watch the current slow down. Be ready to get in as soon as it looks slow enough, because it can speed up again quickly. Every time I've dived at this site the current has been going in a southeasterly direction, whether it was flood or ebb tide. Other divers have reported the same observation to me, but there may be the odd time when it goes the other direction.

Because the current almost always flows from the west to the east, start at the northwest corner and let the current take you in a southeasterly direction. Hang around the western area as long as possible because that is where the life is most concentrated. Along the west-southwest side there is a wall covered in plumose anemones and lots of other life. The wall goes much deeper than I care to venture. My favourite route is to start at the northwest corner and work my way around the outside, onto the wall. There is also a fair bit to see through the channel between the two reefs. The life is not as concentrated when you get to the southeastern area of the reef, but it is still a lot better than most dive sites. See the dashed lines on the map for my two favourite routes to follow.

Depths: You can go as deep as you want along the wall. The channel between the two reefs is about 45 feet deep.

Hazards: The current at this site should not be taken lightly. This is a popular fishing area so watch for boats and hooks.

Other Considerations: Definitely dive with a *live* boat. It's not a bad idea to tow a surface float around with you so that the boat driver knows exactly where you are when you are underwater. If you require a safety stop and the current pulls you off the reef, you can easily drift a long way in three minutes. With a float, your boat will see that you are moving and can follow you as you easily and safely perform your safety stop in mid-water. Discuss all this with your boat driver beforehand.

Rubly Island

Boat Dive

Attractions: A good variety of life and underwater terrain make this a site you will want to do at least a couple of times.

Directions: Use the Sidney boat launch. Rubly Island is at the southeastern tip of Domville Island.

Latitude-48° 39.9'

Longitude-123° 18.7'

Where to Dive: The eastern side of the island is the place to be. There are a couple of small islets just off the east side. Stay on the outside (east) of these islets. It is deeper at the northern end of the island and therefore it is preferable to start at that end and work your way to the shallower southern end.

Sea pen

Current: Slack is a must. In the shallower areas the current is a lot stronger. If the current sucks you into the passage between the island and the two small islets, you could easily get tangled up in kelp. The trick to avoid getting sucked into the shallow passage is to stay at 40 feet or deeper when you are approaching the northern end of the passage. This applies to dives on an ebb tide only.

Depths: At the northern end of the island, the bottom slopes quickly down to 90 feet. At the southern end there are the two islets and there is also a small reef, about 15 metres (49 feet) long, east of the islets. The two islets and the reef beyond them create a valley that is around 50 feet deep.

Hazards: On an ebb tide, the current has a tendency to take you into the shallow passage between the two islets and Rubly Island. The current in the passage is at least twice as fast as in the surrounding area, and in the summer this passage is thick with kelp. Navigating through a kelp forest in strong current is difficult and dangerous.

Rubly Island
Boat Dive

N

60-80 ft.

0-30 ft.   30-60 ft.   Over 80 ft.

Caution!
Very Strong Tidal Currents
Occur Often At This Site

When you are in the area shown to the right, try to keep below 40 feet so that you don't get sucked into the shallow passage. This applies to an ebb tide only.

Rubly Island

Avoid getting sucked into this passage.

0-30 ft.

The dashed line shows the best route to take. I like to start at the north end of the island and work my way south, but the current is not always accommodating.

This Map Is Not To Be Used For Navigation.
Use only as a general guide for diving purposes.

Sidney Area

Other Sites

Boat Dives

Arachne Reef is a pinnacle that rises from the depths. It attracts a fair number of different species of fish. Many times at Arachne I have seen schools of large dogfish circling the pinnacle. It is quite a spectacle.

The best way to dive Arachne Reef is to go down to your maximum depth right away and then spiral your way around the pinnacle as you ascend to shallower depths. The currents at this spot are not particularly strong, but you must dive at slack. It is also best to use a live boat because if your boat drags anchor, it will be gone.

Use the Sidney boat launch and go east around the northern tip of Sidney Island, then around the southeastern tip of Forest Island. Go north between Forest and Gooch Islands. At high tide all that is exposed is the light beacon. Arachne Reef is between Moresby and Gooch Islands.

Latitude-48° 41.1'
Longitude-123° 17.6'

Canoe Rock is a shallow spot where the current runs fast and the life is abundant. Dive at slack, preferably with a live boat. You could dive Canoe Rock at slack and then head over to the *G.B. Church* a short distance away. Canoe Rock is between the northern tips of Moresby and Portland Islands.

Latitude-48° 44.0'
Longitude-123° 20.3'

Cooper Reef is home to lots of seals, especially at low tide. This reef is just north of Gooch Island. Most people go to the HMCS *MacKenzie* instead of this spot, which is a stone's throw away. Dive on the north and east sides at slack tide.

Latitude-48° 40.2'
Longitude-123° 16.5'

Forest Island is a good site for beginners as it is relatively shallow and the current is not terribly strong. Dive along the southwest side.

Latitude-48° 39.6'
Longitude-123° 20.0'

Imrie Island is an average dive with average life, but not a lot of divers go there so it is largely undisturbed. Imrie Island is in the middle of a triangle between Brethour, Coal, and Moresby Islands. There is a shallow reef on the east side of the island. Start at the reef and go

northeast around the north side of the island. Dive at slack.
Latitude-48° 41.7'
Longitude-123° 19.9'

Joan Rock is similar to Arachne Reef in that it is a pinnacle, but it is a little more spread out. There is a float that marks its location. Dive at slack.
Latitude-48° 41.4'
Longitude-123° 19.0'

Little Group Islands is a good dive area for beginners. The current is not too strong and the depths are generally shallow. The northeast side of Dock Island is good. The Little Group is just south of Coal Island or northeast of the town of Sidney.
Latitude-48° 40.3'
Longitude-123° 22.0'

Reay Island is one dive I haven't done yet, so I don't have any details to pass on.
Latitude-48° 40.6'
Longitude-123° 19.7'

Sidney Spit can be either boring or a really good dive spot. Chasing crabs and finding all the treasures strewn about is a lot of fun, but if you are not finding anything and there are no crabs to chase it is just a lot of sand. The constant flow of boat traffic is the reason there are so many treasures here, but it is also a reason for divers to be very careful. Tow a float and a dive flag and don't dive near the dock. A live boat is the best way to fend off other boats. Boats, current, and rope from lost crab traps can all be big hazards.

The sandy bottom is home to lots of sea pens, shrimp, and crabs. If you are after crabs, remember that you are now required to have a fishing licence to collect them. Please adhere to the size limits and don't keep any females.
Latitude-48° 39'
Longitude-123° 20.5'

South Cod Reef is not the same calibre as its big brother, North Cod Reef, but it is still worth a look. You will find it just south of Gooch Island. Dive at slack tide only.
Latitude-48° 39.2'
Longitude-123° 18.0'

SECTION V

Sansum Narrows

Sansum Narrows lies between Saltspring Island and Vancouver Island. The best access to the narrows is either from Cowichan Bay in the south or Maple Bay in the north. Both are in the Duncan area.

The current here does not flow as fast as in some narrows, but it does flow fast enough to provide ample food for a wide variety of marine life. The visibility varies quite a bit, but Sansum Narrows generally isn't one of your better spots for "good vis."

Boat Dives
> Bold Bluff Point
> Burial Islet
> Octopus Point
> Sansum Point

Sansum Narrows
Overview

For more information about the boat launches see the "Boat Launches and Dive Stores" section in the beginning of this book.

Maple Bay
Boat Launch

Boat Ramps

1) Cowichan Bay Boat Launch
   1800 block of Cowichan Bay Road
2) Cherry Point Marina
   Off Sutherland Drive
   Ph. 748-0435
3) Maple Bay Boat Launch
   At the end of Maple Bay Road

Octopus Point

Bold Bluff Point

Sansum
Point

Burial Islet

Cowichan Bay
Boat Launch

Cherry Point Marina

Bold Bluff Point

Boat Dive

Attractions: The rocks are not plastered with life here, but there are abundant and varied life forms, including a good variety of anemones, other than plumose, as well as lots of small fish and a few larger ones. Steep rock slopes and small walls dominate the underwater terrain; large boulders and rocky bottom are also prevalent.

Directions: Bold Bluff Point is on Saltspring Island, across from the halfway point between Cowichan Bay and Maple Bay.

　　Latitude-48° 47.3'

　　Longitude-123° 33.2'

Where To Dive: Start on the side of the point from which the current is coming and drift around the point to the other side, where the current may be weaker.

Current: Dive on slack. On a flood tide a back-eddy sometimes occurs in the bay to the north of Bold Bluff Point. As with many back-eddies, this one can create a current that travels away from the land on both sides of the point. For this reason it is a good idea to use a live boat.

When the current is turning to flood, add 25 minutes to the Active Pass current predictions. When the current is turning to ebb, subtract 35 minutes from the Active Pass current predictions. (Active Pass Current Tables are on pages 74 to 77 of the *Canadian Tide and Current Tables*.)

Depths: I saw the best life in the areas above 80 feet, but it does get deep in a hurry if you want to go a little deeper to explore.

Hazards: Strong and unpredictable current and boats.

Bold Bluff Point
Boat Dive

Over 100 ft.

50-100 ft.

0-50 ft.

The two arrows to the right indicate a possible back-eddy that can occur during or at the end of a flood tide, creating a current that could take you into the middle of the narrows.

Reef

Bold Bluff Point

There is a reef that extends out from the tip of the point. Follow this reef around to see the best life.

Saltspring Island

SANSUM NARROWS

Direction of flood tide

Sansum Narrows

This Map Is Not To Be Used For Navigation.
Use only as a general guide for diving purposes.

Burial Islet

Boat Dive

Attractions: As you drift past the islet you will see areas that have concentrations of different types of invertebrates, the most predominant being small white anemones. There are a lot of sponges, tube worms, and unusually friendly fish.

Directions: Burial Islet is approximately 2 kilometres north of the entrance to Cowichan Bay. Launch from Cowichan Bay and go north into Sansum Narrows or launch from Maple Bay and go south into Sansum Narrows.

    Latitude-48° 46.2'

    Longitude-123° 33.7'

Where To Dive: The northwest (Vancouver Island) side is my favourite. It has the most marine life and the bottom topography is a little more interesting. You can dive the southeast side (the channel between Burial Islet and Saltspring Island), but it is a little flatter and there is slightly less marine life. The reef around Burial Islet is much larger than the islet itself, so you should submerge a fair distance off either end of the islet. A depth sounder can be handy for this. If you don't have a depth sounder, consult your nautical chart before picking a place to go down. The dashed line on the map follows the main area of the reef.

Current: Burial Islet and the surrounding reef are not too big, so if the current is strong you will be past the best part very quickly. Dive at slack time. Remember the current can cruise through at a good pace and can pick up after slack very quickly, so a live boat is best.

    When the current is turning to flood, add 25 minutes to the Active Pass current predictions. When the current is turning to ebb, subtract 35 minutes from the Active Pass current predictions. (Active Pass Current Tables are on pages 74 to 77 of the *Canadian Tide and Current Tables*.)

Depths: The northwest side goes down in ledges to the abyss. The southeast side goes to about 60 feet.

Hazards: Current and boats.

Burial Islet
Boat Dive

Over 120 ft.

90-120 ft.

60-90 ft.

30-60 ft.

0-30 ft.

Marker Light

Burial
Islet

> **Caution!**
> **Very Strong Tidal Currents**
> **Occur Often At This Site**

The dashed line marks the best course to follow. It will take you past the areas with the highest concentrations of life. Don't worry if you get caught in a current and end up going around the inside (east) of the island. It is almost as good.

Saltspring
Island

This Map Is Not To Be Used For Navigation.
Use only as a general guide for diving purposes.

Octopus Point

Boat Dive

Attractions: Although I haven't seen any octopuses at this site, they must be here because I see a lot of crab shells (crab is their favourite food) and there are definitely a lot of hiding spots for them.

The main attraction of this site is the sheer wall that carries on from the towering cliffs above the water down to hundreds of feet underwater. I always get a big thrill when I'm in the water a few feet from the rock, knowing that the water below me is hundreds of feet deep. The wall is covered with anemones and various other invertebrates, and all the life seems to be large: big fish, big urchins, and big anemones, among others.

Directions: Launch at Maple Bay and head out of the bay. Turn south (right) and look to your right to see the impressive-looking cliffs above the site.

Latitude-48° 48.0'
Longitude-123° 33.7'

Decorator crab

Octopus Point
Boat Dive

N

← Maple Bay

Over 100 ft.

50-100 ft.

0-50 ft.

Lighthouse

Octopus
Point

Small
Cliffs

Big
Cliffs

Aquaculture
(Marine Farm)

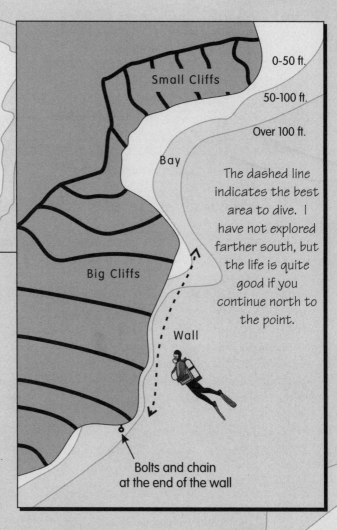

0-50 ft.

Small Cliffs

50-100 ft.

Over 100 ft.

Bay

The dashed line
indicates the best
area to dive. I
have not explored
farther south, but
the life is quite
good if you
continue north to
the point.

Big Cliffs

Wall

Bolts and chain
at the end of the wall

Caution!
Very Strong Tidal Currents
Occur Often At This Site

Sansum
Narrows

This Map is Not To Be Used For Navigation.
Use only as a general guide for diving purposes.

Where To Dive: The best place to dive is not right at the point but a little to the south. Dive near the middle or the north end of the biggest cliffs. There is a large bolt that sticks out of the rock and is visible when tides are about 3 metres (9.5 feet) or lower, which is basically all the time. From the bolt north is the best place to dive.

Current: Dive on slack. There is a current that flows down and out to the middle of the narrows during a flood tide. I experienced this current one day. The surface looked slow enough, but we were a little late and when we got down on the wall the current was much stronger. As we neared the north end of the wall the current grew even stronger and was flowing almost straight down. The moral of the story is: pay attention to current predictions, do not push your time, and dive right at slack. The "downdraft" can be very strong and it is an unsettling feeling (to say the least) to get caught in it. I have also seen the surface current going one direction while a deeper current is going the other way.

When the current is turning to flood, add 25 minutes to the Active Pass current predictions. When the current is turning to ebb, subtract 35 minutes from the Active Pass current predictions. Active Pass Current Tables are on pages 74 to 77 of the *Canadian Tide and Current Tables*.

Depths: The bottom topography is quite varied. Some areas get very deep very quickly, while 100 feet away the bottom may be shallow and sloping.

Hazards: Current and boats.

Sansum Point

Boat Dive

Attractions: A garden of life flows across the bottom on gently sloping hills and along some outlying walls. The bottom is covered with life in a way that you normally only see on wall dives.

Directions: Launch at Cowichan Bay. Go north through the Narrows and past Burial Islet a short distance until you reach Sansum Point.

Latitude-48° 46.8'

Longitude-123° 33.5'

Where To Dive: You can dive right off the point, as shown on the map, or you can dive on the east side of the point where there is a shallow reef. On the east end of the reef is a sloping wall that goes down to about 70 or 80 feet. The wall is covered with plumose anemones and various other life. The wall is at least 180 metres (600 feet) from shore and a long way into the narrows. If you want to avoid a long swim, it is a good idea to use a depth sounder and submerge a fair distance from shore.

Diver exploring a field of plumose anemones

Current: A boiling cauldron of current will greet you when you arrive early to watch it slow down. Make sure you are ready to get in the moment it slows down enough—don't wait for it to stop. On one dive we were not prepared to get into the water; when we did it had already turned. We were only about 10 minutes late, but on a large tidal exchange you are lucky to get 30 minutes of dive time.

When the current is turning to flood, add 25 minutes to the Active Pass current predictions. When the current is turning to ebb, subtract 35 minutes from the Active Pass current predictions. (Active Pass Current Tables are on pages 74 to 77 of the *Canadian Tide and Current Tables*.)

Depths: For the most part the bottom slopes gently. You would have to go a long way into the narrows to get below 100 feet.

Hazards: Extreme current and boats.

Sansum Point
Boat Dive

Caution!
**Very Strong Tidal Currents
Occur Often At This Site**

I would estimate that the current flows four times faster over the shallow reef shown to the right than it does in the surrounding areas.

Reef

Wall

**Sansum
Point**

0-50 ft.

50-100 ft.

Over 100 ft.

The dashed lines indicate the two good routes to follow. I prefer the wall at the east end of the reef, indicated above.

**This Map Is Not To Be Used For Navigation.
Use only as a general guide for diving purposes.**

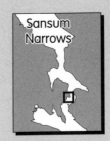

Sansum
Narrows

THE AUTHOR

As a child, Greg Dombowsky was inspired by Jacques Cousteau's incredible portrayals of underwater marine life and knew that when he grew up he would learn to dive. When he did start diving in the late 1980s, he found a need for a book that more thoroughly covered his home base of Victoria. He also concluded that maps specifically created for divers would be more useful than the nautical charts usually included in diving guides. With the purchase of a 17-foot Avon inflatable boat, Greg was able to explore more of the local dive sites. His increasing knowledge of the area, his progress through the PADI ranks, and his growing computer skills (which allowed him to "draw" the maps for the book), gave him the inspiration and confidence to begin writing this book in 1995. Since then he has dived every site in this book at least twice, and most of them many, many times.

Greg comments: *The Victoria area is an incredible place to dive. The marine life here rivals any that I have seen anywhere in the world. By taking my passion for scuba diving to another level by way of underwater photography, I have realized the incredible variety and complexity of marine life that we have here. There are so many world-class dive sites easily accessible from the city, as well as the convenience of many dive shops close by. You can go out for a dive in the morning and be home by noon.*